IN MY FATHER'S HOUSE

Lessons Learned in the Home of a Civil Rights Pioneer

Bob Shands

Bushel Basket Publishing, LLC
Olathe, KS 66062

ACKNOWLEDGMENTS

It would have been impossible to complete this project without the help and support of many people. My wife, Adriane, has been a constant supporter during this process and has devoted untold hours editing and reading the seemingly unending number of re-writes.

Ron Benjamin gave me encouragement to begin this project in 1998. His input led me to choose a viewpoint from which to write.

Many people have been willing to read and provide critical input. My sincere thanks go out to Ken McGovern, Jeff Ostrander, Pete and Roslyn Burney, Larry Brown, Karen Vaughn (my sister) and her husband Tom Vaughn, Donna Knoell, Jim Royer, Harold Lasley, Greg Wegener and Joe Kennedy. Thanks to Greg Pinson for sharing memories. Thanks also go to Joe and Nancy Kennedy for their hospitality in their home as I traveled to Atlanta to conduct research.

Research was obtained through the help of Carolyn Carter of the Auburn Research Library in Atlanta, GA, Cathy Loving of the Atlanta Public Schools Archives & Museum, Rev. Jimmy Moor of St. Mark United Methodist Church in Atlanta, GA, Bishop Bevel Jones III, Peggy W. Mapp of the West Hunter Street Baptist Church in Atlanta, GA, Ethel Ware Carter of the Regional Council of Churches of Atlanta, and *The Atlanta Journal-Constitution.*

Thanks to Diane Wiebe and her husband Chris for the cover design. Thanks to the West Hunter Street Baptist Church for permission to use a picture of the church.

Acknowledgments

Last, but not least, my father, O. Norman Shands, provided personal remembrances and hours of fact checking. More importantly, he and my late mother, Catherine Shands, provided a loving home environment and gave a living example of the love of Jesus Christ.

TABLE OF CONTENTS

ix

PREFACE

I was raised in the South during a turbulent time in our nation's history (1949 through 1963). Many people today say that they cannot relate to stories they hear about the Jim Crow South. Surprisingly, I have heard this from well-educated whites as well as rich beyond belief black athletes. This statement is more frequently heard in my current home of Olathe, KS, a suburb of Kansas City, than in southern regions. The memory of those times must not fade away. It must be kept alive.

Some who lived through those times have advised me against writing this book and have refused requests for memories. Their admonition is "Times were so much different then. That was a long time ago. Leave the past alone." Yet, *The Olathe News* reported on August 23, 2005 that an organization named the Knights of the Ku Klux Klan had distributed flyers the previous week in an attempt to form an organization in Olathe. The aftermath of hurricane Katrina has laid bare racial wounds and differences. Two 13-year-old twins, Lynx and Lamb Gaede, are receiving national attention for singing "white pride" songs under the banner of their band, Prussian Blue. And the voices of two of the giants of the civil rights movement are now quiet following the death of Rosa Parks on October 24, 2005 and Coretta Scott King on January 30, 2006.

My personal views on social justice were shaped by living in Atlanta, GA from 1953–1963. There were three distinctively different, yet powerful, forces molding my consciousness during those years.

First, and foremost, was my home life. My father was a Southern Baptist minister. He was a giant in my eyes. On Sundays I would sit in the second row of the sanctuary at West End Baptist Church and look almost straight up at him delivering the sermon in the pulpit. He seemed almost larger than life. He was a handsome, well-spoken preacher. More a teacher than preacher, actually. No fire and brimstone here. But he was unyielding in his belief that Christians have a responsibility in the area of civil rights. Much of this book will be devoted to my father's activities because they gave me an insider's look at the struggle.

The second major influence on my journey was, in fact, the church. It might seem repetitive to say that in light of my father's activities. However, the information bombarding my psyche at church was very different from my father's teachings. The positions taken by my father were unpopular within the congregation. They were not shared by many of the people who were teaching me in Sunday school. These good people were being challenged by their pastor to reevaluate their thinking about civil rights. It did not go smoothly. There were many car rides home from church business meetings – my mother driving through the tears caused by the anger directed toward my father. The impact on a young boy was tremendous. How could my kind and loving father be so demonized by members of his church – people I loved and admired?

The third influence was the secular society in which I lived my daily life. School, shopping, television. This was a world committed not just to segregation. The commitment was to a worldview that blacks were inferior to whites. There was a fear that life, as we knew it, would come to an end if blacks were not kept "in their place." My friends at school were raised in homes where this view was held as gospel. A sixth grade classmate was the daughter of an Imperial Wizard of the Ku Klux Klan. Other friends' parents were members of the Klan. Even friends whose parents were not active in the Klan, which thankfully included most of my friends, grew up with much different input than did I.

I began this project in 1998 by taping my parents' answers to questions about those days. My original plan was to write something that I would give to my nieces and nephews. I wanted them to have a sense of who their grandparents were. I was unmarried (divorced) and childless. At 49 years of age, I did not anticipate that I would have a child of my own with whom to share these memories.

I procrastinated in starting my project. Two more great-grandchildren were born in 2000, bringing the number to eight. Number nine was born in 2002. The advancing age of my parents and the continued growth of the family should have given me sufficient motivation to begin writing, but it did not. But another event occurred in 2002 that made the project more personal and gave me the motivation I needed.

I was fortunate to marry Adriane Fulson on April 28, 2002. I met Adriane in 2000 when I went to work as an investment representative at the large bank at which she worked. This bank did not discourage workplace relationships. On February 3, 2003, I became a father for the first time. The birth of my son, Bobby, provided the very personal motivation that I needed to begin writing.

Adriane is a beautiful and talented African-American woman. Bobby is bi-racial. Adriane also had four children previous to our marriage. At the time of our marriage, there were incidents in our county of cross burnings and racially specific graffiti at homes of minorities. My father asked me if I were prepared for what might occur as we injected our racially mixed family into our new neighborhood. My mind dredged up memories of Dad's unpopularity in Atlanta in the 50's. The only response I could make was "Are you kidding me?" This book will explain how I came to make that response.

CHAPTER 1
SETTING THE STAGE

My family moved to Atlanta in March of 1953.
My father began his new work as pastor of the
West End Baptist Church on Easter Sunday,
April 5th. He had just celebrated his 37th birthday on March
13th. I had turned four years old in late January. Dad was
returning to the pastorate after having served a little more
than one year as president of Limestone College in Gaffney,
S.C. Prior to his presidency of Limestone, he had served his
first full-time, large congregation as pastor of the First
Baptist Church of Spartanburg, S.C. from 1947 to January of
1952. I was born in Spartanburg in 1949.

Limestone was a private Baptist woman's college.
As the youngest child of the school president, the students
doted on me. I have joked, frequently, of life's cruelty that I
couldn't have been older during my father's tenure there. I
remember that the attention I received from the girls (as they
were called at the time) made me very shy. I was constantly
hiding behind my mother's skirts. The fact that we were at

Limestone for such a short time was a blessing as far as memories are concerned. I remember much of that year. I know that any memory I have of Limestone would have occurred during the year in which I was three years of age.

I vividly remember the day we moved from Gaffney to Atlanta. I rode with my father. My older brother and sister rode with my mother. The intent was that the two cars would stay in close proximity to each other. At one point, Mom stopped for gas, and Dad did not realize it since he was in the lead car. To say that Dad panicked might be an exaggeration. But he was very concerned. Mom had not been driving long, having learned to drive in Gaffney. Dad stopped at a Highway Patrol station to inquire of accidents the officers might have heard of on their radio. Because of this stop, Mom caught up with us; and we all arrived in Atlanta at the same time.

This was the first time I witnessed Dad's strong concern at times when Mom was "out of place." It was not the last. Mom ran all of the errands for the family, including the "taxi service" for the kids' activities. Sometimes Dad would arrive home while Mom was still out. It always seemed to me that his reaction was over the top. He would call the police and hospitals. He would call the neighbors. I came to realize, in my adult years, the reason for his behavior. And to appreciate that it was not over the top at all.

My first memory of the house was of a small green counter top in the kitchen next to the refrigerator. It was across the room from the main countertop and the sink. There was no furniture in the house, of course. It was still on the moving van, which would arrive later in the day. We ate our first meal in the house on that countertop, standing as we ate. Later that afternoon, I went to the grocery store with

Dad to pick up a few necessities. The grocery was a Colonial Store. Across the street was a five and ten store. I was to spend a small fortune at that "dime store" on baseball cards in later years.

Bob on the back porch of his childhood home
in Atlanta, GA at the age of eight.

Our back yard was deep and pie shaped. There was a canopy of tall pine trees, almost totally blocking the sun. A carpet of pine needles covered the ground. The only grass was at the very rear point of the lot. On one side was a white wooden fence that ran the length of the yard, separating our yard from the neighbor's yard. A boy my age, Steve Baldwin, was standing on one of the rungs of the fence. I immediately ventured over and made my first friend. Moving was not turning out to be so bad. Later that day, I met another boy my age, Greg Pinson, who lived across the street. This was going to be great!

Atlanta in 1953 was not the metropolis that it is today. True, it was one of the South's largest cities, but it was not considered "major league". Major league sports would not arrive until 1966 after the construction of a new multi-purpose stadium. The Braves were still in Milwaukee. In fact, the only professional sports team in Atlanta was the Atlanta Crackers, a minor league team of the Milwaukee Braves. Football fans got their fix by focusing on Georgia Tech and the University of Georgia.

Atlanta was a banking center. Although Georgia Tech was originally a textile school, Atlanta's industry was not dominated by textile mills, as were many other Southern cities. The major manufacturer was Coca-Cola – a very clean industry in comparison to the steel city of Birmingham, AL and the paper mills of South Georgia.

The pace of life was glacial in comparison to today. Interstate highways were almost a decade off. Air conditioning was unheard of in my neighborhood. No one had air conditioned homes or cars. Televisions were black and white. There were three stations – NBC, CBS and ABC. In fact, we did not even own a television at the time of our move. I remember the day Dad brought our first television home. It must not have been too long after we reached Atlanta. The television shows I watched were Roy Rogers, Gene Autrey, the Mickey Mouse Club, and of course cartoons – Mighty Mouse, Felix the Cat, Tom and Jerry, Mickey Mouse and Donald Duck. The family shows were Ozzie and Harriet, Father Knows Best, the Gale Storm Show and Perry Como.

My world was very white. Obviously, there were blacks living in Atlanta. I would see blacks in public places.

Places like train and bus terminals. There were occasional rides on public buses. I would see blacks then. They sat in the back of the bus, behind a white line painted on the floor near the rear exit door. Many families had black domestic help. But, day in and day out, I had no contact with blacks.

Catherine, Norman, Karen, & Bob Shands talking with a church member (far left) after moving to Atlanta.

As a "PK" (preacher's kid), much of our time was spent at church. There were no black members of our church. As I grew older, school took a large portion of my time. There were no black students in my schools. There was a wonderful public swimming pool not far from our house in the John A. White Park. Blacks were not allowed in the public swimming pools.

Much has been written about the Jim Crow era in the south. Jim Crow laws purported to provide separate but equal facilities. Nothing could be farther from the truth. The passage of time coupled with the migration of northerners to major southern cities has sanitized the memory of those days in the nation's eyes.

The "equal" public facilities were nothing of the sort. The public restrooms available to blacks were beyond filthy. "Colored" water fountains were indeed colored. They were beige porcelain. They were not cleaned as often as the white fountains. Southerners did not believe that there was anything equal about blacks.

My father told me of a conversation with the Executive Secretary of the South Carolina Baptist Convention, a gentleman named Simms. In his youth, Mr. Simms had heard the deacons of his church debate whether blacks had souls. These conversations occurred under a shade tree on the church property. Because Simms was approximately fifteen years older than my father, these conversations probably took place around the turn of the 20th century.

Children have no concept of time. The Civil War was ancient history to me. In reality, it had not ended all that long ago. Adults in Atlanta had grandfathers who had fought in the Civil War.

The loss of the Civil War meant an end to an entire culture. Slavery was the economic underpinning of that culture. Cotton, tobacco and rice were the principal crops in an agricultural society. The crops were planted and harvested with slave labor. The profits were reaped by white society. While there are many reports of benevolent slave owners, even the best of them considered other human beings – black human beings – chattel. Many slave owners were not benevolent. I think the only way to rationalize the horror of owning another person was to consider the "property" less than human, or at least inferior.

Mary Shands Jordan with
Bob and her other grandchildren.

I have had the luxury of visiting with my father many times during the writing of this book. He made a statement to me in one of the times I was struggling with the positions taken on race relations by some members of the clergy. He said, "A fish is not aware of the water. It is simply a given of the environment." I'm sure that whites born into a culture of slavery took it as a given. Just as the inferiority of blacks seemed to me to be a given in white Atlanta.

It would have been difficult in those days for a child to come to any conclusion other than black inferiority. Children are very aware of people in certain professions: policemen, firemen, teachers, preachers, and bankers. These are the jobs to which children aspire. No white child in Atlanta in the 1950's would have seen a person of color in any of those professions.

Blacks held the menial jobs: janitors, garbage collectors, cooks, maids, waiters (in some restaurants). This reinforced the perception of inferiority. It was almost as if slavery had never ended. Blacks still performed the dirtiest jobs. They were now paid something for their efforts. I'm sure that most whites considered this great progress for Negroes (one of the two polite ways of referring to African-Americans).

But for me, a 4-year-old white boy, life was very good in Atlanta. I had no way of knowing the turmoil that the next decade would bring for my family, my church and my city.

CHAPTER 2
THE CALM IS SHATTERED

The Brown vs. Board of Education of Topeka Supreme Court decision on May 17, 1954 shattered the relative calm in Atlanta. The decision, read by Chief Justice Earl Warren, stated, "We conclude that in the field of *public education* (italics added) the doctrine of 'separate but equal' has no place. Separate educational facilities are inherently unequal"(Essential Documents in American History 1492–Present). While the decision applied only to public education, the true effect was the beginning of the end of segregation and Jim Crow laws.

I try to imagine what that pronouncement would have meant to a person of color living in the Deep South at that time. I have a sense of how I would have felt. I believe that I would have felt as though I had been tightly bound by chains for years. Wrapped round and round, pinning my arms to my torso – squeezing the breath out of my being. All of a sudden the chains are now loosing. Not a lot. But just enough to provide a little wiggle room. Just enough to give me thoughts that I might actually free myself with enough straining and contortion. I know that once the idea of freedom implanted itself in my mind, there would be no room for other thoughts.

The Brown decision did not address the issue of how or when to eliminate forced segregation in education. Chief Justice Warren spoke of this in the decision ". . . the consideration of appropriate relief was necessarily subordinated to the primary question – the constitutionality of segregation" (Essential Documents 1492 – Present). A second Brown decision was announced on May 31, 1955. The court instructed school boards to move "with all deliberate speed" in implementing policies to end segregation in public schools.

Charles J. Ogletree, in his book All Deliberate Speed: Reflections on the First Half Century of Brown v. Board of Education writes:

> As Thurgood Marshall and other civil rights lawyers pondered the second decision, they tried to ascertain what the Court meant in adding the crucial phrase "all deliberate speed" to its opinion. It is reported that, after the lawyers read the decision, a staff member consulted a dictionary to confirm their worst fears – that the all deliberate speed language meant "slow" and that the apparent victory was compromised because resisters were allowed to end segregation on their own timetable. These three critical words would indeed turn out to be of great consequence, in that they ignored the urgency on which the Brown lawyers insisted. When asked to

14

explain his view of all deliberate speed, Thurgood Marshall frequently told anyone who would listen that the term meant S-L-O-W (Ogletree, 2004, p.10).

The issue of public school segregation was a decidedly Southern one. In 1954, law in seventeen southern and border states (Alabama, Arkansas, Delaware, Florida, Georgia, Kentucky, Louisiana, Maryland, Mississippi, Missouri, North Carolina, Oklahoma, South Carolina, Tennessee, Texas, Virginia, West Virginia) and the District of Columbia required that elementary schools be segregated. Four other states (Arizona, Kansas, New Mexico and Wyoming) had laws permitting segregated schools, but Wyoming had never practiced school segregation (The Columbia Electronic Encyclopedia, 2005).

In Atlanta, the capitol of Georgia, the political machinery lurched into gear. On November 2, 1954, a constitutional amendment was adopted providing for a private school system. John W. Letson, the Superintendent of Schools in Atlanta, wrote about those times in the December 1963 issue of the *NEA Journal*.

> Georgia – and Atlanta – reacted to the 1954 in much Supreme Court decision the same manner as did other Southern states and cities. General indignation was translated into massive resistance laws which required the closing of white schools that accepted Negro pupils (In Atlanta Schools, p.46).

Also in 1955, a movement began to change the Georgia state flag to incorporate the Confederate stars and bars. A law to that effect was passed on February 13, 1956. A debate began in the late 1980's over the wisdom of changing the state flag to remove the stars and bars. Initially, I was opposed to any change. I felt that it was an attempt to change history. The Civil War had, in fact, happened, and the Confederate flag was part of that history. I learned, during that debate, that the addition of the stars and bars was made as a protest against the Brown decision. I was appalled and somewhat embarrassed. This caused me to change my opinion and side with those in favor of changing the flag. The flag was altered in 2001. The state seal took prominence. But there were small depictions of other flags that had flown over Georgia and the United States. Included among them was the 1956 version, which included the stars and bars. Another change occurred in 2003, finally vanquishing all references to the Confederate flag.

The decidedly Southern nature of the segregation issue was demonstrated on March 12, 1956 with the presentation in the United States Senate of "The Southern Manifesto". It was signed by nineteen senators, representing eleven states – all Southern. The Brown Supreme Court decision was decried. States, which had declared the intention to resist forced integration through all lawful means, were commended. And a pledge was made to use all lawful means to effect a reversal of the decision. One paragraph of the manifesto stands out above all others, however:

> This unwarranted exercise of power by the Court, contrary to the Constitution, is creating chaos and confusion in the States principally affected. It is destroying the amicable

relations between the white and Negro races that have been created through 90 years of patient effort by the good people of both races. It has planted hatred and suspicion where there has been heretofore friendship and understanding. (Congressional Record 84th Congress, 1956).

The full text of the Southern Manifesto is attached as Exhibit A.

I assume this statement means that whites felt African-Americans were agreeable to riding in the back of the bus; being refused admission to restaurants; and using filthy public restrooms. Such arrangements having been worked out by "amicable relations" and "patient effort". This manifesto was presented by Senator Walter F. George of Georgia. Credit for the final draft of the document has been given to Senator Richard B. Russell of Georgia (Our Georgia History, 2001–2005). Senator Russell had previously led a successful effort in the Senate in 1938 to defeat legislation that would outlaw lynching (Our Georgia History, 2001–2005). Another tactic in "amicable relations" and "patient effort".

Three Southern Senators did not sign the manifesto: Al Gore, Sr. and Estes Kefauver of Tennessee and Lyndon B. Johnson of Texas.

The Southern Manifesto makes it clear that, in the chaos, blacks no longer "knew their place." In later chapters, I discuss the economic importance to the South in keeping blacks in the menial and low-paying jobs – "their place."

In addition to mobilizing the political machinery, another consequence of Brown was the revival of the Ku Klux Klan. Atlanta had long been a center of Klan activity. David Chalmers book, <u>Hooded Americanism: The History of the Ku Klux Klan</u> tells of the special relationship between Atlanta and the Klan. "For fifty years, Imperial Wizards have come to Atlanta to take up their reigns" (Chalmers, 1981, p.70). According to Chalmers, the suburb of Stone Mountain was considered hallowed ground by the Klan.

> One of the major themes in the history of the Ku Klux Klan in the twentieth century has been its long-lived relationship with the state of Georgia. The Klan was reborn there in the fertile mind of Colonel Simmons and consecrated on the top of Stone Mountain, which for almost fifty years has been sacred soil for the Invisible Empire (Chalmers, 1981, p.70).

Stone Mountain is a city at the base of a large block of granite protruding from the red Georgia clay. Local lore claims that it is the largest single piece of granite in the world. It is large enough that it requires a ski lift to reach the top. On one side is a Mount Rushmore type carving depicting Robert E. Lee, Jefferson Davis and Stonewall Jackson. All are on horseback.

The Klan had its beginnings in Pulaski, TN in December of 1865. Most histories of the Klan report that its original incarnation was brief – ending in 1871. It experienced two major revivals, one in 1915 and another in 1946. Both took place with speeches and cross-burnings on top of Stone Mountain. The first revival was led by Colonel

William Simmons. It coincided with the release earlier in the year of the film *The Birth of a Nation* that romanticized the actions of the original Klan. "The Ku Klux Klan was depicted as the savior of the white race against the ravages and criminality of the black race" (Quarles, 1999, p.53). The movement flourished across the South until the beginning of the Depression.

Dr. Samuel Green, an Atlanta obstetrician, led the second revival. Chester L. Quarles, in his book The Ku Klux Klan and Related American Racialist and Antisemitic Organizations, cites historian Robert P. Ingalls' account of the October night in 1946:

> On the appointed night, a mob of Klansmen climbed to the top of Stone Mountain for the naturalization (induction) ceremony. The way was lit by a fiery cross, measuring 200 by 300 feet, on the side of the mountain. A shortage of hoods forced hundreds of Knights to wear handkerchief masks. However, in all other respects, the initiation followed the pattern set down by Colonel Simmons in 1915 (Quarles, 1999, p.83).

Quarles attributes the success of the 1946 revival to "a new assertiveness on the part of the Negro race" (Quarles, 1999, p.83). Blacks who fought in World War II were returning with the idea that their service merited an improvement in civil rights. In addition, they had not experienced in Europe the racial prejudices that existed in the South. There were no "colored" water fountains and European women were not averse to dating black American soldiers. The Klan thrived until the death of Dr. Green in 1949.

The Ku Klux Klan of the twenty-first century is generally considered a fringe organization – fractured into several sects. The Klan of the mid twentieth century in Atlanta was no such thing. Leonard Pitts, the insightful columnist for *The Miami Herald*, wrote a tribute to the renowned African-American actor, Ossie Davis, upon Davis' death. It was published in the Kansas City Star on February 15, 2005. In it, Pitts refers to Davis "having grown up in Georgia at a time when the Ku Klux Klan was virtually a shadow government" (*Miami Herald*, 2005). Chalmers gives a vivid example of this shadow government at work. In his book, he publishes the minutes of a Klan meeting on November 1, 1948.

Meeting of Atlanta Georgia, Klavern No. 1
November 1, 1948

125 present
10 new applicants
1 reinstatement

The Grand Dragon, Dr. Green, has had all of his teeth pulled, and consequently was not feeling well. He came but didn't stay long. He let R__ act, as Exalted Cyclops, in his place.

Rev. H__, an old railroad engineer, made a long talk on a visit he had with Senator Russell, who promised that he would have Congress pass Federal laws to prohibit intermarriage between black and white. H__ made a religious talk that in God's sight it is no sin to kill a nigger, for a nigger is nothing more than a dog or a beast. Russell told him he had one of his books, and he was going to use his book and the same scripture passages to pass the bill against intermarriage.

H__ is to preach to-morrow (Wednesday) night at East Point and it is to be broadcast and all Klansmen are invited to listen in or attend.

Jimmy H__, the city detective, spoke about a white man who was shot by a nigger last Friday – or perhaps it was by two niggers. He said they knew whom and would arrest them. He also spoke of a Negro and a white man arrested in Carrollton, Georgia, for the murder of a white boy . . . whose body was found in some bushes. The boy was trying to protect the girl whom he was going with from being attacked by a mask-wearing man. The girl said she was sure it was a colored man. H__ said this was about the fourth attack lately in that vicinity and it looked like the Klan was going to have to do something around there. He said about 1,000 people were milling around the jail in Carrollton yesterday, trying to take the nigger out and lynch him.

B__, the Grand Titan, talked. He said this showed how great the need was to have a Klavern in every community, because of such attacks.

A policeman named C__ got up and made a long talk along the same lines.

Trigger N__, also a policeman, got up and made a talk and said he hoped he wouldn't have all the honor of killing the niggers in the South and he hoped the people would do something about it themselves; and that Carrollton had some good Klansmen in it who were able to handle the situation – but maybe they needed some help from the outside and if some went up (from No. 1) to put on a parade or demonstration it might help things out.

R__ and V__ (head of the Klavalier Klub) reported on Videlia. Said 300 attended and they were met by the Chief of Police, the Assistant Chief, and the Sheriff of the County (all of whom gave their assistance). Everyone of the city officers are Klansmen, except the Mayor who is opposed. The Klan has said that it will have a new Mayor after the next election. They are going to work on him. Dr. Green made a speech (from Videlia) and it was broadcast throughout South Georgia.

In the West End, where there has been trouble with the Negroes buying property and moving in, a fellow named H__ reported colored people buying up real estate and moving in on Glenn Street and around Candler Warehouse. R__ said he would have the Klavalier Klub investigate.

R__ said Drew Pearson did not have anyone in the Klavern Hall to give out information, any more. He commented on Drew Pearson quoting Dr. Green's urging all Klansmen to vote for Thurmond. Also, he said, the man who gave out that information was out of the Klan for good. He referred to this man as a "bald-headed bastard."

R__ urged all Klansmen to get out and get the vote in Tuesday morning and to work like they did in the last primary – when working for Talmadge – for Thurmond (Chalmers, 1981, pp. 330–332).

Drew Pearson was one of America's leading journalists and did, indeed, have an informant in the Klan in Atlanta. Stetson Kennedy was a Southern writer who infiltrated the Klan. The Klavalier Klub was an elite flogging squad to which he gained admittance. Kennedy later wrote a book <u>The Klan Unmasked</u> and testified against the Klan in many courts of law.

Whereas Chalmers abbreviated last names in his account, Kennedy does not. Trigger N__ was probably Trigger Nash. Kennedy writes about a Klan meeting as follows in which the Imperial Wizard dumped the contents of a small carton onto his purple hood:

"Now for something a little different," he said. "I have here fifty .45 caliber Police Special Revolver cartridges. I'm putting them up for auction, minimum bid one dollar each! The proceeds will go towards our political action fund. It cost us a lot of money to get rid of that Jew Henry Morgenthau as Secretary of the Treasury, and now we are out to get rid of that Catholic Francis Biddle as Attorney General! The Klan is applying pressure at the proper places to clean Jews and Catholics out of high Government places. We all feel that Truman will do his best to help us.

He's firing F.D.R.'s Jews and niggers as fast as he can. Now what am I bid?

After the auction was completed, the Imperial Wizard had an idea involving Nash.

"I have a suggestion to make," he said, rapping for order. "Why don't we contribute these cartridges to Brother Itchy-Trigger-Finger Nash? He knows what to do with them." Shouting their enthusiasm, the Klansmen who had acquired the cartridges came forward and deposited them in Nash's police cap.

"I'm much obliged," Nash said modestly, "but I hope I don't have to kill all the niggers in the South without getting some help from my Brothers!"

"Don't worry – you'll get plenty of help!" a number of Klansmen shouted.

"In God's sight it is no sin to kill a nigger, for a nigger's no more than a dog!" The Klud intoned piously from his station.

"I will say one thing," Nash concluded. "Chief Jenkins has put me on the day shift on the [Atlanta] Police Force, so I can devote my nights to riding with the Klan!" (Kennedy, 1990, pp. 65–66)

Nash's comment about Chief Jenkins may well have been braggadocio. Herbert Jenkins became Chief of Police in 1947 with the pledge that he would reduce KKK influence in the department (1996–2004 City-Directory). He served in that position until 1972. But the fact that the pledge was necessary demonstrates the degree of Klan infiltration.

Talmadge was Herman Talmadge. He was elected in 1948 after having been elected in a special election in 1947 to fill the term of his father, Eugene Talmadge. Gene Talmadge died in 1946 after winning that year's election only to die before he could take the oath of office. It would have been his fourth term as Governor. Both Eugene and Herman had close affiliations with the Klan. Eugene pardoned six imprisoned KKK floggers in 1941 and Herman appointed Dr. Green aide-de-camp on his staff in appreciation for Klan political support (Chalmers, 1981).

Stetson Kennedy reported a public statement that Samuel W. Roper of Klavern 297 hade about Herman Talmadge before the 1948 election. Roper was probably "R__", referred to in Chalmers' Klan meeting minutes.

> I thought the Brothers might be interested in a little talk I had with Talmadge last week. I asked him what he thought was the best method of keeping niggers from voting. He didn't say anything but picked up a scrap of paper and wrote one word on it: "pistols!" He also promised me that if elected he would give the Klan a free hand in any race rioting, before call in the Militia!" (Kennedy, 1990, p.64).

Herman Talmadge later rewarded Roper by appointing him to head the Georgia Bureau of Investigation (Chalmers, 1981). Roper was himself 25-year veteran of the Atlanta police (Kennedy, 1990). Upon Dr. Green's death in 1949, Roper became Imperial Wizard. According to Chalmers, splinter groups had sprouted during Green's reign, but he had succeeded in suppressing them. Roper's leadership was not as strong, and the Klan split into many smaller factions. Membership dwindled creating what I previously referred to as a period of relative calm.

Chalmers and Quarles each give the Brown ruling credit for giving the Klan another jolt of energy. Eldon Edwards, a paint sprayer at an Atlanta automobile manufacturing plant, had organized his Klan in 1953. His partner was James Venable, a Stone Mountain attorney and Klansman of long standing. Edwards' Klan was floundering until the 1954 Supreme Court decision (Quarles, 1999). By 1958 Edwards' Klan numbered 12,000 to 15,000 members. His was the largest of at least seven other Klan organizations across the South (Chalmers, 1981). In all, there were over 100,000 new Klan members in the South (Rice, 1962). And these Klansmen were violent.

In 1959 the Friends' Service Committee, National Council of Churches of Christ, and the Southern Regional Council published a report on the first four years after the Brown decision. The title was *Intimidation, Reprisal and Violence in the South's Racial Crisis.* Chalmers listed the following incidents culled from 530 acts of violence cited in the report:

6 Negroes killed;
29 individuals, 11 of them white, shot and wounded
    in racial incidents;

44 persons beaten;

5 stabbed;

30 homes bombed; in one instance (at Clinton,
   Tenn.) an additional 30 houses were damaged
   by a single blast; attempted blasting of five
   other homes;

8 homes burned;

15 homes struck by gunfire, and 7 homes stoned;

4 schools bombed, in Jacksonville, Nashville, and
   Chattanooga, and Clinton, Tenn.;

2 bombing attempts on schools, in Charlotte and
Clinton;

7 churches bombed, one of which was for whites; an
   attempt made to bomb another Negro church;

1 church in Memphis burned; another church stoned;

4 Jewish temples or centers bombed, in Miami,
   Nashville, Jacksonville, and Atlanta;

3 bombing attempts on Jewish buildings, in Gastonia,
   N.C., Birmingham, and Charlotte;

1 YMCA building in Chattanooga and an auditorium
   in Knoxville dynamited;

2 schools burned;

In addition, 17 towns and cities were threatened by
   mob action (Chalmers, 1981, pp. 349–350).

The bombing of the Jewish Temple in Atlanta occurred in October1958 and was attributed to the support Rabbi Jacob Rothschild had given to the desegregation of the public schools. Some people felt that the media had paid little attention to the bombings of African-American homes prior to the bombing of the Temple (Retrenchment and Redirection 1950–1959, 2004).

But, just as the Brown decision had energized government and the Klan, the African-American community was energized as well. In 1955, Rosa Parks was arrested in Montgomery, AL for refusing to give up her seat to a white man on a city bus. The Montgomery bus boycott began, and racial issues began to be discussed on the evening news broadcasts. Also in 1955, the NAACP held a convention in Atlanta. It urged local chapters to pressure school boards to adopt the Brown decision and desegregate.

The entire social structure of the south was being turned upside down. It was in this environment that my secular socialization began. In the fall of 1954, I would be attending kindergarten. The thoughts expressed by my classmates would actually be the thoughts expressed by their parents. I would hear things that were much different than I was being taught in my home.

The things I heard were vile. One of my earliest memories of racial discussions with my peer group involved the "colored" water fountains. I was told that, if you drank from one, you were not getting water. You were getting recycled nigger spit. This caused me to gag every time I passed a colored fountain.

This was one of the insidious ways that messages were transmitted to me regarding racial issues. Another was simply the use of the term "nigger". It may have started as an example of the lazy southern lip's attempt at Negro. That is not the way I remember the use of the word.

Nigger. This word was not a noun. It was not an adjective. It was an indictment.

In the politically correct 2000's it seems attempts are made to pretend this word never existed. If someone lets it slip, we politely say, "He said the N word." Some African – Americans even seem to use it as a term of endearment. But

I have no interest in sugar coating the greater society in which I was raised. I can think of no word of greater contempt that I have heard in my 56 years.

There is an image at times of a kindly southern plantation owner using the word in a somewhat benign way toward his slaves. Having their best interests at heart, etc.

The way I heard the word used conjures up a far different memory. It was a word that had to be delivered with a good measure of scorn. Strong emphasis on the first syllable. It was as if blacks would cease to exist if the word could be delivered just the right way. "Abracadabra" and POOF, they would disappear.

It was not a word with which I was unfamiliar. It seemed to permeate our society. Classmates used it without much thought. There was no shock in the hearing. No shame in the utterance. Blacks were simply considered inferior beings. There had to be a word that would sufficiently identify them as such.

There was talk at school about the fact that we could someday be attending school with "n_____s". Very few people I knew, outside of our home, referred to African-Americans as anything other than n_____. My best friend, Greg Pinson, and I rarely talked about racial issues. Greg has said that his parents did not talk of such things. Both of our families had maids. Of course, they were colored. I knew of no one who had Caucasian domestic help. Greg's mother treated their maids very courteously. Therefore, most of the vile messages I received were delivered at school.

At home, the talk around the dinner table, supper as the evening meal is called in the south, increasingly turned to God's love for all people. In the years to come, the prayer before supper would include supplications that God would forgive those who would wish to harm us. I assumed that this was because some of the things Dad said in sermons made some church people mad. I had no idea until years later the extent to which Dad became a public figure and put himself and our family at risk.

CHAPTER 3
GEORGIA BAPTISTS
1956

In My Father's House

The year 1956 witnessed an escalation of racial tensions in the South. The Southern Manifesto was presented in Congress. The Montgomery bus boycott that began on December 5, 1955 lasted virtually the entire year, ending on December 21, 1956. The year also was the year of "coming out" for Dr. Martin Luther King, Jr.

When Rosa Parks refused to give up her seat on a Montgomery, AL bus for a white man on December 1, 1955, Dr. King was pastor of the Dexter Ave. Baptist Church in Montgomery. Dr. King was one of the organizers of the bus boycott. He was also elected President of the newly formed Montgomery Improvement Association. On January 30, 1956, his home was bombed. When he arrived at home, an angry, armed crowd of African-Americans had formed. He sent them home with the advice, "We cannot solve this problem through retaliatory violence. We must meet hate with love" (Johnson and Adelman, 2000, p.16). Thus began the non-violent movement for social change.

The year 1956 also was a year in which I began to be aware of events. It was the first New Year's Day that I remember. I didn't like how "1956" looked or sounded. It lacked the symmetry of 1955. I actually missed 1955. I turned seven years of age the day before Dr. King's home was bombed. In the fall, I entered the second grade at a brand new elementary school, West Manor Elementary. We hadn't moved. A new school had been built to alleviate overcrowding. I was more aware that friends from church were also friends at school: Tom Ingram, Tim Heard, Mike Lawrence, Billy and Cathy Geren. My best friend continued to be Greg Pinson – the boy who lived across the street. We never had classes together at school, however. We are sure that our mothers conspired to have us assigned to separate classes, at least until we entered high school.

My interest in and awareness of girls increased, as well. I was not one of those boys who thought girls were "yucky". I had an interest in a girl in each of my kindergarten and first grade years. But I actually had a "crush" in second grade. Her name was Debbie. She was blonde. And the days she wore her Brownie uniform were very special.

I also began to take an interest in professional sports. I became aware of Mickey Mantle during the World Series of 1956. My first baseball glove was a Mickey Mantle version. I became a fan of the Washington Redskins. I watched them religiously, pun intended, every Sunday. It was the southernmost team in the National Football League. As such, their games were televised to Atlanta weekly.

Coincidental with my year of "awareness", 1956 also represented my father's "coming out" in the battle over school desegregation.

Otis Norman Shands

      In 1956, Dad was serving on the Social Service Commission of the Georgia Baptist Convention – having served as Vice-President of the convention the previous year. This commission had been established in 1911 as a "standing commission to promote temperance, law enforcement and other social and moral reforms" (*The Atlanta Constitution*, November 13, 1956, p.3). The Brown decision had thrown the issue of school desegregation into the arena of law enforcement and social and moral reforms. Southern Baptists were the largest religious denomination in Georgia with total membership of 800,000.

The annual meeting of the Georgia Baptist Convention was held in Atlanta in November of 1956. The hot topic of this convention was to be a report of the Social Services Commission on the issue of school desegregation. The commission consisted of the chairman, Rev. Judson G. Jackson, LaGrange, GA; Rev. Henry J. Stokes, Macon, GA; Rev. John B. Burch, Savannah, GA; and my father. The commission was originally constituted of five members, but one had left the state during the year.

A front-page article in *The Atlanta Constitution* on Tuesday November 13, 1956 reported that the commission had released an advance text of its report to be delivered at 9:45 a.m. the following day under the headline "**Baptists Air Bid to Back Integration**". I can think of no more inflammatory headline for the time.

Evidently, only three members of the commission were in agreement with the report. Rev. Burch was quoted in the article as having been unable to attend the final meeting of the commission and had not seen the full report.

The following portion of the article, along with full text of the commission's report, appeared under the subheading "**Expect Objections**":

> The church commission of four members, only three of which participated in the report, recognized differences of opinion

on the issue and said it received conflicting advice on what stand it should take.

It anticipated the possibility of further sharp objections but said, "Certainly hateful words and deeds and scornful denunciations of those who differ with us is not the Christian way of solving this problem . . . neither will silence and inaction on our part solve it.

In reciting "some things which we feel would greatly help" it listed:

1. Recognizing difficulties involved, we should exercise Christian grace and patience with one another.

2. We should faithfully teach and proclaim the basic Christian principles that apply to the problem such as the universality of Christ's gospel, "good tidings of great joy, which shall be to all people" . . .

3. To accept the Supreme Court decision as the law of the land and acknowledge that it is in harmony with the constitution and our fundamental democratic concepts and with principles of our Christian religion.

4. We can through our churches seek to create an atmosphere that would make it possible for those who administer our public schools to comply with the instructions of the courts.

5. As other Christian groups share these convictions with us we can strengthen our witness by cooperative effort to raise the level of our knowledge, sympathy and

understanding of our mutual problem and obligation. This can be done by supporting such organizations as the Georgia Council on Human Relations, formerly called Georgia Committee of Interracial cooperation. This is an old organization established in 1919 under the leadership of such men as our own Dr. Ashby Jones. It has at the present time as its executive director, Dr. Guy H. Wells, a Baptist who has given most of his life in the field of education in Georgia.

Baptist leaders were not amused. Another *Atlanta Constitution* front-page headline on Wednesday, November 15th declared "**State Baptist Leader Sees Integration Veto**". The article quoted Rev. A.B. Hawkes of Waycross, Ga., saying that he did not believe the convention would approve the report. Rev. Hawkes had served as chairman of the administration committee of the Georgia Baptist Convention for three years.

Rev. Burch, the member of the committee quoted in the previous day's article as not having seen the report, distanced himself from the rest of the committee. He was cited in the article as refusing to approve points three and four that specifically dealt with school desegregation. Other delegates quoted in the article seemed to be split on the chances of approval by the full convention of the report.

On Wednesday, November 15, 1956, Rev. Jackson, the Social Services Commission chairman read the report to the general session of the convention. My father and Rev. Stokes both took the floor to speak in favor of acceptance of the report. Thursday's *Atlanta Constitution* headline announced "**Baptists Reject Motion To Accept Race**

Ruling". The article was continued on page 8 under the headline "**Race Clause Tossed Out By Baptists.**" A picture of my father appeared on this page with the caption "Must Face Issues".

The rejection of the report was overwhelming. The margin was 3 to 1. The article gave credit to Rev. John B. Burch of Savannah and Dr. Louie D. Newton of Atlanta as spearheading the decision. Rev. Burch specifically made a motion that sections 3, 4 and 5 of the report be deleted. It should be noted that this is not the John Birch for whom the John Birch Society was named.

Rev. Burch "said these recommendations were not in keeping with my own personal convictions". He added he did not believe the "race relations section can contribute to the solution of the problem."

Dr. Newton was quoted as saying that he was prepared to make the same motion as made by Rev. Burch. "Dr. Newton expressed his belief these recommendations would put an added burden on ministers, laymen and laywomen who are already seeking a solution to the explosive situation." Dr. Newton was pastor of one of Atlanta's largest Baptist churches – Druid Hills Baptist Church. Prior to that, he had been editor of *The Christian Index,* the state denominational newspaper. He was powerful in Baptist circles and had attained the moniker "Mr. Baptist". Most often, he was simply referred to as "Louie D". As will be seen in Chapter 5, he was also extremely well connected politically. To this day, Mercer University in Macon, GA annually bestows an award bearing Dr. Newton's name to the Baptist in Georgia who has performed outstanding service to the university.

Dr. Newton and my father both graduated from Mercer University. Dr. Newton was approximately the same age as my grandfather who died in 1933. Dr. Newton's brother was a doctor in Macon and delivered my older brother who was born while Dad was a student at Mercer. Dr. Newton called Dad an idealist – which Dad took as a compliment. I have never heard my father utter any negative word toward anyone other than a Republican politician. He was always a defender of Dr. Newton while my mother expressed her outright disdain when his name was mentioned. The occasion of the 1956 convention was the first time Dr. Newton and my father would disagree over the issue of school desegregation. It would not be the last.

In addition to soundly defeating the resolution of the Social Services Commission, the convention took the additional step of increasing the number of members of the commission to fifteen so "the true feeling of the convention would be represented." This quote was attributed to Rev. J. Thornton Williams of Forsythe GA., the chairman of the convention's nominating committee.

The further step was taken of limiting the commission's annual report to 500 words. The *Constitution* article said that the report of the commission "produced the stormiest session thus far in the three-day convention meeting at the First Baptist Church . . ."

In preparation for the writing of this book, I shared my research of this convention with my father. He responded, "I didn't realize how out of touch with the mainstream I was."

The next Georgia Baptist Convention, in 1957, was to be held in the relative obscurity of Valdosta GA at the far south end of the state. The 1956 convention was held in Atlanta. It produced front-page headlines in the South's largest newspaper. Dad was the only supporter of the report whose picture was published and to whom a quote was attributed.

> Dr. O. Norman Shands, Atlanta, commission member speaking in favor of the report, said there is a "moral obligation on Georgia Baptists to face every moral issue associated with the racial problem." He added he did not believe Christians should "hedge".

He was also the only member of the Social Services Commission who lived in Atlanta. I am surprised our home was not bombed that very evening.

But, while the Klan and church members were taking notice, so was the African-American community. The first indication of this came in the form of a letter to my father from Whitney Young who would later become president of the National Urban League in 1961. In 1956, he was a professor of sociology at Atlanta University. In his letter, Mr. Young indicated that he had been very pessimistic that leadership on racial issues could come from white churches. He stated that the actions of the Social Services Commission, while unsuccessful, gave him renewed hope of the possibility of that leadership.

Other forward-thinking people took notice, as well. The week following the convention, Dad received a telephone call from Harry Rohrer, a past Executive Director of the YMCA for the state of Georgia. He invited Dad to lunch at which they discussed creating a forum for the open discussion of racial issues. The Shands-Rohrer Club was formed. Meetings were held semi-monthly at the Atlanta YMCA. Invitations were extended to the president of the NAACP, the president of Atlanta University, Rabbi

Rothschild of the Jewish Temple and many other clerical and lay leaders.

My father had placed himself, and by extension our family, center stage in the racial turmoil in the South's largest city. Threats of violence would follow. The immediate threat, however, would be the reaction of the members of West End Baptist Church.

CHAPTER 4
WEST END BAPTIST CHURCH

West End Baptist Church was founded in 1888. The congregation moved into the building at 1040 Gordon Street in September of 1952. The building was only 6 months old when we arrived. I was not aware of the newness of the building until I began researching this book. The concept of "new" probably doesn't register with a 4 year old. I do remember that the funds to erect a steeple had not been available, giving the façade of the building the look of a "flat top" haircut. But that hairstyle was very much in vogue for men in the 1950's.

Many people have the idea that PK's (preachers' kids) are mischievous and rebellious. I was neither. Sure, it had its drawbacks. Lots of "thou shalt nots" and fewer material possessions than most of my friends' families. But I loved being the preacher's youngest child. I was doted on, just as I had been doted on at Limestone College.

One of the perks of being a PK was being in the church on weekdays when visiting my father at his office. The building would be virtually vacant except for the occasional whine of the floor buffer on days the floors were being polished. I have not been in the building since the mid-sixties. Yet, I think I remember every square inch.

The sanctuary was beautiful. There was a center aisle. Dark green marble columns ran along the side aisles, which separated the main seating from side seating under the side balconies. There was also a loft balcony in the back. The carpet was a medium shade of green. The pews and all of the woodwork were a medium shade of brown. Lighter than mahogany and darker than pine. The pews were not cushioned.

West End Baptist Church

My family's place during worship services was on the second pew to the left side of the sanctuary as one faced the pulpit. The pulpit was raised meaning Dad could look almost straight down on us and just to his right. On the rare occasions I misbehaved enough to be removed by my mother for a spanking, the whole church could see. This led me to grow up with the idea that God was always watching along with 3000 eyes.

West End (the area) had actually been a city at one time (Historic West End, 1981). It even pre-dated Terminus, which was the first name for Atlanta. There are numerous references in my research to a change in the racial makeup of West End beginning as early as the mid 1940's.

The church address was 1040 Gordon Street, now named Ralph Abernathy Blvd. The immediate neighbor to the west was a museum named the Wren's Nest. This had been the home of Joel Chandler Harris. He was a past editor of the Atlanta Constitution and was the author of the Uncle Remus stories. Some of my earliest knowledge of blacks came from watching cartoons of Uncle Remus characters on Disney. The dialect of the black storyteller, Uncle Remus, was difficult to understand and emphasized to me the differences between blacks and whites. What little contact I had with blacks included seeing some older blacks out in public. Many of them still talked in this slave dialect. In my child's mind, these differences were inherent.

The Wren's Nest was now a museum. A female member of our church was the curator. Admission was charged and souvenirs were sold. There was a large back yard that was accessible from the church parking lot by climbing through a tall hedgerow. My fourth grade class performed a Dutch dance in this yard complete with bloomered pantaloons and wooden shoes. And of course Dutch boy caps. A lady in our neighborhood on Highview Road sewed my blue costume.

Between this large, green back yard and the main house was a building that had been the slave quarters. I hated going into this building. It was dark. The ceilings were low. Everything was cramped. I cannot fathom that somehow it had been permissible for humans to keep other humans living in such quarters. This was my most direct connection to time of slavery.

The people of West End Baptist Church were wonderful to me and, for the most part, to my father and mother. As I stated earlier, these were people whom I respected, admired, and loved. Many were parents of my best friends. The names and faces come flooding back. Most of the memories are wonderful. The major source of conflict was over my father's position on desegregation and civil rights. Not all members were in conflict with Dad. I could sense the genuine love that most had for my parents. I knew the specific positions of few of them. My parents tried to minimize the conflicts and rarely talked about individuals. Most references were to "the deacons". In that way, my parents successfully shielded the children from much hurt.

But it was clear that the official position of the church was a segregated position. The members were Southerners. And, as my father said, a fish is not aware of the water. I mean no disrespect to the membership of West End Baptist Church in the writing of this book. The few members I did disrespect shall remain nameless.

Prior to the events of November 1956, there had been one serious attempt by a Negro to worship at our church. That occurred on July 13, 1954. Of course, that was not long after the Brown decision. On that Sunday morning, prior to the Sunday school hour, a black man arrived at the front entrance to the church intending to worship that day. This alarmed the men of the church who came to my father in his study. Dad instructed the men to bring the gentleman to his office.

The visitor explained that he was a Pentecostal minister, currently unemployed. He said that when he woke up that day, the Lord had laid on his heart that he was to worship at West End Baptist. He expressed a concern about racial attitudes at the church and quoted a couple of scripture verses. Dad agreed that there was much progress to be made in the area of treating each other as Christian brothers and sisters.

My father told him that he was on his way to teach a men's Sunday school class. He invited the gentleman to come along. Dad introduced him to the class as his visitor and invited him to give his Christian testimony. Dad then taught the class, and the visitor participated in the discussion.

On the way to the sanctuary for worship, Dad invited the minister to worship, again as his guest. He would ask the minister to sit on the front pew near the pulpit. At the time of welcoming of visitors he would introduce the visitor as his guest. Dad told him that he would not be able to invite him to give his testimony because of time constraints. We would be observing communion, "The Lord's Supper" as Baptists called it, at the end of the service. In addition, our services were broadcast on the radio each Sunday, which required that they be finished in a specific amount of time. Dad did, however, tell the minister that there would probably be some commotion and disagreement because of his attendance.

The minister declined the invitation to attend the worship service. He said that the scriptures teach that we should do all things decently and in order. It would not be decent or orderly of him to cause a strain between Dad and the congregation because of his attendance. This was especially true because he felt that he had been treated as a brother in Christ. He expressed his appreciation and left.

In the following days, there was some criticism of my father. A group of people, including a few deacons, was close enough to hear the final conversation between Dad and the minister. They did not think Dad handled the situation properly. There was also criticism of Dad's position on race relations in general.

Prior to the Georgia Baptist Convention in 1956, Dad had not made a point of preaching about race relations. However, he would express his views if they were in context with the scripture verses around which some sermons were built.

His positions had caused the deacons to attempt to quiet him on one earlier occasion. A motion was made at a meeting of the deacons to instruct the pastor to refrain from preaching on "controversial subjects". This motion was made at a meeting that took place while my father was not in attendance. He was out of town preaching a revival service. Southern Baptist churches usually had two revival meetings a year. This involved a worship service every night of the week. The speaker for the week was a pastor from another church or, perhaps, a professional evangelist.

Someone had the good sense to move that the motion be tabled until the next deacons' meeting so that Dad could be in attendance. At the end of the following month's meeting, it was pointed out that there was a motion that had been tabled and needed to be acted on.

Upon hearing the motion, Dad asked that Roberts Rules of Order be dispensed with and he be allowed to speak from his heart. He said that if he were merely an employee of the church, he would feel the need to comply with any instruction of the deacons. But he felt that the fundamental basis for his hiring at West End was in the context of being called by God, and led by the Holy Spirit, to preach the Gospel as he saw it. And to provide leadership to the church. He acknowledged his duties to the deacons in the light of a higher calling that he felt they also acknowledged upon his hiring.

The discussion was open, frank and mutually respectful. The motion did not pass.

After the meeting, Dad was approached by one of the deacons, Jimmy McGarrity, Sr. He told Dad that he had disagreed with him more times than he had agreed. Dad responded that he was aware of this. Jimmy then said, "But you are my pastor. Would you pray for me – that I would become a better Christian?" Dad answered that he would if Jimmy would agree to pray the same prayer for him.

The highly public events of the Georgia Baptist Convention caused an explosive reaction within the church.

In the 1950's, a man's identity was defined by where he worked and where he attended church. Today, we live in such a transitional society that it is difficult to imagine a time in which men worked at the same company for 35 years and attended the same church most of their lives. Few women worked outside of the home. The men of our church were being confronted at their places of work about Dad's notoriety.

The Chairman of Deacons, John Still, came to visit my father in his office after the convention. He said that many of the church members, including deacons, were asking him, "What do you think of your nigger-lovin' preacher now?" Dad asked John how he had been replying. John said, "I don't always agree with him, but he's my pastor". Dad felt that this was the most appropriate response he could give.

John Still was a man I looked up to. He taught teenage boys in Sunday school. My older brother, Norman, had talked fondly of John from his time in Sunday school. John was the Treasurer of Fulton County. He was a sophisticated and learned man. His family always treated my family kindly and warmly.

West End Baptist Chairman of the Deacons, John Still (right), reviewing a document with two other deacons.

Early in 1957, a special meeting of the deacon board was called to deal with my father's activities at the convention. A motion was made that the deacons should recommend to the church that the pastor be "censured". Of particular concern to some deacons was that Dad had publicly taken positions that were opposed by Louie D. Newton, "Mr. Baptist". It was no small matter to be publicly opposed by Louie D. Newton.

I can just hear the workplace taunts endured by our church members. "My pastor, Louie D., doesn't hold such n_____-lovin' views".

The special meeting of the deacons was chaired by John Still. John began the meeting by making some personal comments. He said that he was a Southerner in all of its meanings and contexts. He read a letter written by his grandfather from a battlefield in the Civil War. He told of having been present at a lynching in his youth.

He then said that he had taken three days vacation from work to prepare for this meeting. He had visited *The Atlanta Constitution* and the Atlanta Public Library to read materials on racial issues – usually referred to as "the Negro problem". He had thought of scripture texts that he had taught to the boys in Sunday school. He had thought of some of my father's sermons. He then stated that he had decided that the thoughts, ideas, and precepts he had held all his life were not consistent with the Gospel of Jesus Christ. He offered his resignation as chairman of the deacon board.

This was greeted with calls of "No, John. Don't resign". John proceeded to break down in tears. In embarrassment, he retreated to a small classroom off of the main room in which the deacons were meeting. Dad joined him, and together they prayed.

After regaining his composure, John returned to the meeting, where discussion had continued. He said, "You may throw stones at Dr. Shands, but you will have to throw them at me, too, for I will be standing between him and you. He is my pastor".

This defused the anger in the room. In my father's opinion, it also saved his job. The motion was made and died for lack of a second. The pastor was not censured.

Some thirty years later, John's wife, Cybill, lay in a hospital bed in Atlanta in very serious condition. Almost overcome with grief, John went outside to sit in the sunshine. He must have looked very sorrowful because a large, buxom black woman passed by on the sidewalk and stopped to ask John why he looked so forlorn. John told her of his wife's medical troubles. This woman then pulled John to her breast, stroked his head and told him to not worry. She told him to go back inside and be with his wife. Everything would be okay. He started off and realized that he had not thanked the woman. He turned to thank her, and she was nowhere to be seen. It was if she had disappeared.

John found Cybill awake and alert. Her crisis had passed.

Upon telling this story to my father, John asked Dad if he believed in angels. Dad answered that yes, he did. John then asked Dad why God would send him a black angel. Dad's response was that it was probably just what John had needed at the time.

CHAPTER 5

THE CHURCH IN CRISIS

Whitney Young was not the only person who took notice that leadership in the area of civil rights was not being offered by the "white" church. The 1956 Georgia Baptist Convention had been held at the First Baptist Church of Atlanta. This was one of the three largest and most influential Southern Baptist churches in Atlanta. The pastor was Dr. Roy McClain. The worship services were televised each Sunday. Dr. McClain would have been actively involved in the sessions of the convention as the host pastor. Early in 1957, Dr. McClain preached a sermon in which he addressed the Christian's responsibility to confront prejudice.

Dr. McClain had penned the words that became the "catch phrase" for the sermon in a book published in 1957, This Way Please: Facing Life's Crossroads.

"Herein Christians must share in the responsibility for such universal prevalence of prejudicial thinking; if not for its inception, then surely for its continuity, by tolerating it in side-stepping silence and encouraging the deception that it will work itself out if given time. This no more is the case than that weeds will uproot themselves by their own initiative. Public utterances are comparatively easy, but encountering a prejudiced individual on the field of verbal combat is a challenge from which most Christians are prone to shrink. *There are times when silence is golden; there are also times when silence is yellow!* (emphasis added) (McClain, 1957, p.156).

Ralph McGill, the progressive editor of *The Atlanta Constitution*, took note of Dr. McClain's sermon. He issued an invitation to a number of Protestant ministers to write their own position papers on the segregation issue. The church was being "called out" to take a stand on the most pressing social issue of the day. For the most part, it was found wanting.

I have long thought that churches in the first half of the 20th century, and before, performed a social/entertainment function. In the days before movie theatres, radio and television, the entertainment choices were the local bar or the local church – especially in rural communities. I bristled as a child at the countless hours spent at church. Church school and worship services on Sunday morning. Church school and worship services on Sunday night. A social hour after the Sunday evening service. Organized door knocking (visitation) on Tuesday evening. A church supper on Wednesday evening followed by more church school and another worship service called "prayer meeting". Then there were the semi-annual revival meetings. Worship services every night of the week for at least one and sometimes two weeks with a guest preacher. Dare I say entertainer. How I envied my friends who were Methodists or Presbyterians. They didn't have to go to church on Sunday night or Wednesday night.

Unfortunately, the Ku Klux Klan had also recognized the entertainment function that the church served. The Klan revival of 1915 had been led by Colonel Simmons. Simmons had washed out as a Methodist minister prior to reviving the Klan. Chalmers gives the following account of the close relationship between the Klan and the church.

> Released from the army, inspired by patriotism and Americanism, too poor to study medicine, he turned to the career traditionally open to talent, the church. It was not a happy choice but it was a useful one in developing his talents. The ministry did not pay. He rode circuit and was given only backwoods districts in Alabama and Florida, never the big churches, such as Mobile or Montgomery for which he yearned. He developed his oratory and his eloquence, and gave popular lectures at revival meetings on "Women, Weddings, and Wives", "Red Heads, Dead Heads, and No Heads", and the "Kinship of Kourtship and Kissing." And he went deeper and deeper into debt on his $200 to $300 yearly stipend, each year attending the

church conference with hopes that this would be his year to get the 'big' church. The bishops of the Methodist Church South, however, recognized their man. The call was missing, and they failed to move him upward.

After twelve years, the 1912 Alabama Conference voted to deny him a pulpit because of inefficiency and moral impairment, and he was pushed out to tread the secular path to fame and fortune." (Chalmers, 1981, p.29).

Simmons, however, must have recognized that there were others in the ministry who had a secular view of their calling in addition to the spiritual. Not only did the Klan perversely use scripture to justify their white supremacist rants, they were quite effective in using the church as an instrument of their message. Quarles articulates this as follows:

During the period from 1944 to 1950, it was not at all unusual for Klansmen to enter a church sanctuary during a worship service and offer gifts of money to the church. In studies of the Klan, one rarely finds an example of a pastor or church leader turning down an offering of this type. This may well have been true because in some areas of Klan predominance, the leading deacons, elders, or members of the board of trustees were Klansmen themselves. Klansmen would not often go to a public place where they stood more to lose than they stood to gain. Many pastors were concerned, however, about the Klan and sought direction from their denominational leaders.

Dr. Hugh A Brimm, executive secretary of the Social Services Commission of the Southern Baptist Convention, requested all pastors in his denomination do the following in case their services were interrupted by Klansmen bearing gifts:

(1) Keep cool – no one should be afraid of cowards who will not show their faces.
(2) Remember that superficial piety is hypocrisy before God and man. These men cannot wash the bloodstains of lynched victims from their skirts by merely walking into a church with "blood money."
(3) Refuse any gifts and invite them to stay only if they remove their masks. If they refuse to unhood themselves, then dismiss the service with a prayer for them that they might see the light of God's love for all men and themselves come to love all men. (Quarles, 1999, p.85)

Chalmers describes the Klan's recruitment efforts during the Simmons years:

The usual Klan pattern was to approach the local Protestant minister. He would be offered a free membership and urged to take office in the to-be-formed local, either as its chaplain (Kludd) or higher up the leadership structure. Hundreds upon hundreds did join, and in some areas constituted a major portion of the local officialdom. Others left their flocks for the wider Klan calling as either organizers or speakers. Almost all of the national Klan lecturers were ministers. Usually the presence of a Klan in town was announced by a parade of hooded horsemen down Main Street, a cross blazing on a nearby hillside, or a sudden appearance in the midst of the Sunday service. Robed in white, masked, they would divide into three columns and march silently down the aisles congregating in front of the pulpit to present a purse of thirty-five or forty dollars to the minister. If their appearance was not completely unexpected or unwelcome, they might file into the front rows that had been left vacant, while the minister or one among them propounded the principles of the Klan and read from the Twelfth Chapter of Romans, calling upon them to present their bodies, through the Klan, as "a living sacrifice, holy, acceptable unto God." Or, having made the donation, they might march out again while the church choir sang "The Old Rugged Cross" or "Onward, Christian Soldiers." (Chalmers, 1981, pp.34–35)

This was a side of the church I never saw. I was quite surprised and troubled upon locating this information as I did research for this book. Somewhat in denial and hoping to hear something contradictory, I asked my father if this was really true. "Oh, yes", was his immediate response. Hugh Brimm had been on the staff at Mercer University while Dad was a student. Dad had never personally witnessed it. He had grown up in the Eastern Heights Baptist Church in Columbus, GA. It had not happened there during his teen years of 1929 – 1936. It never happened in the small rural churches he pastored in Georgia and Kentucky during his school years because "most people knew that they would not be well received in my church." This indicated to me that he was on record as a very young pastor.

In response to Dr. McClain's call to action, a group of approximately thirty to thirty-five like-minded Protestant ministers met at the Atlanta Club in downtown Atlanta. My father was one of those ministers. Dr. Herman "Chubby" Turner, a senior Presbyterian minister had a church member who was a member of the Atlanta Club and allowed the ministers access. Dr. Turner paraphrased Benjamin Franklin in saying "Gentlemen, we can hang individually or hang together." The ministers decided that they should draft a joint statement on the racial issue. The group elected a committee of nine to draft a position paper.

The draft committee consisted of Dr. McDowell Richards, President of Columbia Seminary, Dr. Turner, Rev. Milton Wood, Dr. Harry Fifield, Dr. Monroe Swilley, Rev. Robert E. Lee, Rev. Harrison McMains, Dr. Charles Allen and Dr. Dow Kirkpatrick. Dr. Richards was credited with being the author of the document, or "our Thomas Jefferson" as one pastor put it. These men were chosen because, in most cases, they served the largest congregations in their denominations. At least the largest congregations whose pastor was willing to sign the document.

Upon completion of the original draft, the full group reconvened. After a few revisions, the position paper was ready for publication. The goal of this group was to obtain the signatures of as many of Atlanta's ministers as possible. Much effort was made to keep the activities of this group secret, given the political climate in Atlanta at the time. Bishop Bevel L. Jones, III was a young Methodist pastor of the Audubon Forest Methodist Church. Bishop Jones, in his book One Step Beyond Caution: Reflections on Life and Faith, gives the following account of how the signatures were obtained:

> Almost as important as the document itself was our method of gathering support for it. We decided not to mail it, for our adversaries could get hold of it and sabotage our efforts. Instead, the clergy comprising our core group glued the manifesto to tables at several designated churches. Then we wrote a letter to all Atlanta area ministers whose addresses we could obtain, asking them to go by and read our manifesto, and if they would support it, to sign their names (Jones III, 2001, p.104).

Meanwhile, the pressure on the church was continuing. Ralph McGill wrote a front-page editorial in *The Atlanta Journal and Constitution* on Sunday September 22, 1957 titled "Dilemma of The Christian." He pointed out that much of the foreign missions money of churches in the South was going to missions in "Africa, Asia, the Orient and South America". Missionaries were having difficulty explaining the images of black children being spat on as they attempted to attend white schools. "The Communist nations, of course, are making great use of it, saying it proves out claims to Christianity and democracy false. For the Christian, the issue is inescapable".

Dr. Roy McClain also kept up the pressure. On Sunday, October 6, 1957 he preached a sermon in which he asked the question "Who speaks for the South? College professors have been 'relatively quiet'. Many of the South's politicians are interested only in getting votes, and the 'pulpits have been paralyzed'". *The Atlanta Journal* printed excerpts of the sermon in an article on the front page the following day, October 7, 1957.

Ralph McGill picked up on the "pulpits have been paralyzed" phrase and invited a number of area pastors to write an article for the paper. The first article appeared the following Sunday, October 13, 1957 in *The Atlanta Journal and Constitution* and was written by Dr. McClain. Between the headline and the body of the article was an editor's note as follows:

> Editor's note: "Pulpits have been paralyzed ... the well-informed people have been quiet." That comment on racial tension came from the pulpit of Atlanta's First Baptist Church last Sunday. *The Atlanta Journal and Constitution* thereupon invited ministers of many faiths to write down the guidance they would give their people on this question. This newspaper's columns will be *(illegible)* on successive Sundays to one of these articles, so that spiritual counsel may have its widest play. Leading off the series is the minister who made the charge of pulpit paralysis, Dr. Roy O. McClain.

Each week, for thirteen successive weeks, an article was printed. A complete list of the ministers, the dates of their articles and their headlines are presented in Exhibit B. Four of the nine members of the committee to draft the joint ministers' statement wrote articles for the series: Dr. Fifield, Dr. Kirkpatrick, Rev. Lee, and Rev. McMains. My father was one of the thirteen. The entire text of his article is presented in Exhibit C.

In this environment, the document that would be known as The Ministers Manifesto was acquiring signatures and being prepared for release. On Sunday, October 27, 1957 *The Atlanta Journal and Constitution* ran an article announcing that a statement on the race issue would be released to the public in the paper the following Sunday. Dr. Turner was identified as the chairman of the committee. He said it was the work of several ministers "on an independent basis, and without reference to any denomination or church council." A member of the drafting committee was quoted anonymously as saying that the document "was written following informal meetings of 'about 35' Atlanta ministers of different denominations. Dr. Turner said that the attempt to garner signatures was ongoing.

The Atlanta Ministers Manifesto of 1957 was front-page news in *The Atlanta Journal and Constitution* on Sunday, November 3rd. "Eighty Atlanta ministers have signed a manifesto presenting the first such declaration of beliefs on racial problems to come out of the Deep South." The article pointed out that the signers "do not include a majority of the white Protestant clergymen, but the group includes pastors of many of Atlanta's largest churches and many longtime leaders of various denominations." Six basic principles were enumerated in the article:

1. Freedom of speech must at all costs be preserved
2. As Americans and as Christians, we have an obligation to obey the law.
3. The public school system must not be destroyed.
4. Hatred and scorn for those of another race, or for those who hold a position different from our own, can never be justified.
5. Communication between responsible leaders of the races must be maintained.
6. Our difficulties cannot be solved in our own strength or in human wisdom . . . but only through prayer.

The entire text of the manifesto was published on page A-6 along with the names of the eighty signers. The text and list of signers is also presented as Exhibit D in this book.

Reaction to the manifesto was mostly positive among other clergy. *The Atlanta Journal* ran a front-page story the following evening under the headline "**Ministers Rallying to Race Manifesto.** Many pastors from around the state were quoted as saying they would have signed it, given the opportunity. There was some negativity. Two Baptist groups, the Colquitt County Baptist Association and the Tatnall-Evans Association were reported in *The Atlanta Journal* on November 8th as taking stands in favor of segregation. The Associated Press polled thirteen of the eighty ministers, all of who reported that there was little unfavorable reaction among their congregations. This was reported on the front page of *The Atlanta Journal and Constitution* on November 10th. The article did point out, however, that some negative letters were received from people outside of their churches. Dad was one of the thirteen quoted in the article.

Bishop Jones gave an account in his book of the reactions he experienced. I imagine that it was fairly representative.

> It was Sunday, November 3, 1957, and I didn't know what to expect at our young Audubon Forest Church on the corner of Sewell and Willis Mill Roads in southwest Atlanta. Many of our parishioners had moved out of West End to avoid living among black people. I had recruited most of them personally, and served among them for eight years. They knew of my concern about race relations. I had spoken out often on the issue, always speaking the truth in love. Many of them disagreed with my stance, but respected me nonetheless.

> I received a number of cold stares that morning as the congregation gathered. Several members asked some serious questions, although none was antagonistic. The general public reacted more aggressively. My phone rang often in subsequent days, and I received letters so hot I needed asbestos files. A few of them reflected adversely on my ancestry (Jones III, 2001, pp. 104–105)

Outspoken clergymen of Atlanta, instrumental in issuance of declaration of Christian Principle are (front row, from left): Dr. Monroe F. Swilley, Jr., Dr. Harry A. Fifield, Dr. Herman L. Turner. Rev. Milton L. Wood. In back are Dr. Charles L. Allen, Rev. Harrison McMains, Dr. Dow Kirkpatrick, Rev. Robert E. Lee. Declaration was first conceived by Alabama-born Dr. Turner, minister of Covenant Pres. Church. The 80 ministers who have signed it are all white.

The manifesto drew national attention. *Life Magazine* published a picture of the draft committee sans the author, Dr. Richards, on November 11, 1957. *Life* referred to the manifesto as ". . . a declaration of working Christian principles that may prove a landmark in southern history. In a state whose leaders have vowed to fight the Supreme Court's school desegregation decision to the bitter end, the ministers made this bold challenge: 'Resorts to violence and to economic reprisals as a means to avoid the granting of legal rights to other citizens are never justified.' *The Atlanta Journal* reported on January 1, 1958 that R.T. Sutcliffe, a

New York Lutheran radio broadcaster, had named the manifesto third among the top ten religious stories of 1957.

Perhaps the most important reaction came from the Interdenominational Ministers Alliance of Atlanta, which represented virtually every black church in Atlanta. *The Atlanta Journal and Constitution* reported on Sunday November 10, 1957 that the alliance had issued a statement thanking the signers of the manifesto. Their statement included the following points:

> 1. Acceptance of the overture for the maintenance of communications between responsible leaders of both races in a search for a solution to racial problems.
> 2. A belief that discussion will reveal methods of solving race problems that are best adapted to different sections of the country.
> 3. Present disunity between the races is largely due to a diversity of opinions about the best methods of handling race issues.
> 4. The church is society's conscience and democracy is not just a system of government, but also an orderly coexistence of people and races within a community or country.
> 5. Both races need to re-evaluate the need for friendship and understanding in these critical times.

There were, however, voices in the African-American community that belittled the effort and impact of the Manifesto. Dr. Benjamin Mays, the president of Morehouse College, said that it was disgraceful that it took white ministers 42 months to come up with a statement that was weak and inconclusive and that could easily have been signed by a segregationist (Moor, 2004). Dr. Martin Luther King, Sr. in his book, <u>Daddy King:, An Autobiography</u> is on record that no white minister ever took a stand to lead his congregation in the area of social justice.

> As early as the 1930's, though not at any time before that, the South might have addressed and solved the nation's racial dilemma. But this would have required a leadership the South did not really *ever* (my emphasis) develop – leadership among white clergymen. Every effort that Negro churchmen made toward not only a reconciliation but also a progressive unity within the framework of southern religious life was rejected. There were simply no white ministers who would run the risk of meeting with us because such gatherings would have to be meetings between equals. The spiritual prison of segregated life was so strong that even the most powerful white minister would have lost his congregation for suggesting that the races were, in the sight of God equals. If this implies that southern whites felt stronger in their faith in racial separation than their belief in the possibility of racial harmony, the record speaks clearly. From the white Baptist churches of the South – and they were and remain the most influential institutions in this part of the country – no one emerged to look at the human condition as it was in the South and to say: Enough, this will come to an end

because it contradicts every part of the Bible and all the doctrine and principles that book contains. We sought out a leader from the white community, feeling that if even one would speak, a new mood could be created here. We discovered that in this instance seeking brought nothing. And so we waited, feeling that across the huge but senseless divide, *someone* (King's emphasis) from the large, heavily populated other side would stand up and be counted, even if just one. It did not happen (King, 1980, pp. 103–104).

Later in his book, in a segment dealing specifically with events in Atlanta in 1957, Dr. King wrote "How sad it is, for example, that not a single white southern minister emerged to influence the spiritual development of whites living though the end of an old order and the start of a new one!" (King, 1980, p. 159).

But blacks, as represented by Dr. Mays and Daddy King were not the only ones who belittled the Manifesto. The Southern Baptist Convention had an employee, Victor Glass, dedicated to fostering good relations between the National Baptist Convention (blacks) and the SBC (whites). Mr. Glass told my father that the Manifesto was weak and didn't cover nearly enough ground.

Dad has told me, however, that the signers of the Manifesto felt they were taking significant professional and personal risks. They were hopeful that the Manifesto would make an impact on race relations and the discourse on school desegregation. Bishop Bevel Jones characterized the effort to publish the Manifesto this way:

In My Father's House

> There come times when each of us must decide whether to risk whatever we have attained and take a stand that is unpopular but morally imperative. When I review my half-century in the ministry, I derive more satisfaction from a step I took in 1957 than just about anything else in my professional life (Jones III, 2001, p.98)

During the week following the publication of the Ministers Manifesto, *The Atlanta Constitution* ran an article on November 8th written by George Connell, the religion writer for the Associated Press. In the article, under the headline "Dixie Baptists Struggle with Racial Anxiety", he articulated the risks – particularly to a Southern Baptist minister – of taking unpopular positions on the racial issue. The basis for the article was an interview Connell had conducted with Dr. Porter Routh, the Executive Secretary of the Southern Baptist Convention. Connell wrote:

> In this heavily Baptist territory of prevailing segregation, with federal courts pressing for integration in public schools and services, which way are Baptist leaders exerting their local influence?
>
> "I'm sure that the great majority of our ministers, and of our Southern Baptist members *in their best moments* (emphasis added), believe in the worth, dignity and value of every individual'" Dr. Routh said.
>
> However, when it comes to particular steps for integration – in schools, church or elsewhere – strong community feeling makes

73

it risky to advocate such a course from the local pulpit.

Some pastors have been ousted on these grounds.

Unlike most other denominations, a Baptist congregation can fire its pastor as quickly as it can take a vote."

One signature of a Southern Baptist pastor was notable in its absence on the Ministers Manifesto – that of Louie D. Newton. The Associated Press article of November 10, 1957, which reported on the reactions of thirteen congregations, pointed out this fact:

Two of Atlanta's best-known ministers declined to sign the manifesto. Dr. Louie D. Newton, pastor of the Druid Hills Baptist Church, said he doubted the wisdom of the statement but hoped it would do "lots of good". He said the declaration had some implications which would raise questions rather than settle them.

The article went on to say that Dr. Pierce Harris, pastor of First Methodist Church also declined to sign the manifesto on the grounds that "he didn't think the declaration means much one way or the other".

During the writing of this book, I asked my father if he could explain how he and Dr. Newton had come to different opinions. His answer was "A fish is not aware of the water." Dr. Newton was a product of an earlier generation. Segregation was to the South as water was to a fish. Dr. Newton's father was born in 1850 and would have been a ten-year-old boy at the onset of the Civil War. Dad said that, for him, the issue of the "racial problem" was one of moral conviction. For Dr. Newton, it was one of politics.

I did not understand that explanation until I obtained a copy of <u>Louie D.: A Photographic Essay of "Mr. Baptist,"</u> <u>Louie DeVotie Newton</u> by Jack U. Harwell. Mr. Harwell was the publisher of *The Christian Index*, a position previously held by Dr. Newton. It is a pictorial history of Dr. Newton's life and career to that date. It should be noted that there are no page numbers in the book. All pictures appear in chronological order by year. I have either listed the people with Dr. Newton in each picture or quoted the caption for the picture. The following pictures appear in the book:

> 1932: Gov. Eugene Talmadge et al.
> 1942: Gov. Ellis Arnall and Mayor William B. Hartsfield
> 1943: Gov. Ellis Arnall
> 1943: Gov. Ellis Arnall and Mayor William B. Hartsfield
> 1958: Mayor Hartsfield et al.
> 1962: Gov. Ernest Vandiver et al.
> 1964: Gov. Carl Sanders and Mayor Ivan Allen, Jr.
> 1971: "Louie D. led funeral procession bearing the body of the late United States Senator Richard B. Russell of Georgia, a longtime friend. Funeral was at Georgia Capitol Rotunda".
> 1971: Gov. Jimmy Carter and Roslyn Carter
> 1972: President Richard M. Nixon, Mrs.

Patricia Nixon, Congressman Carl Vinson, and Gov. Jimmy Carter

1976: Griffin Bell (Attorney General in the Carter Administration) among others

1976: "Louie D. interviewed Rosalyn Carter, Mrs. Lillian Carter and Gov. Jimmy Carter on WGST radio station in Atlanta. Louie D. interviewed many leaders during 50 years on WGST".

1976: "Louie D. was greeted by President Rufus C. Harris and U.S. Senator Herman Talmadge as Mercer University gave Louie D. its Bicentennial Distinguished Alumnus Award."

1976: Gov. George Busbee among others

1977: "This letter from President Jimmy Carter was read as Atlanta Baptist Association paid special tribute to Louie D."

As I previously mentioned, Eugene Talmadge, Herman Talmadge, and Richard Russell enjoyed a particularly close relationship with the Klan. Senator Russell led the "Southern Bloc" of Senators in 1938 to defeat an anti-lynching bill supported by the NAACP. Ernest Vandiver was elected Governor in 1958 on a segregationist platform. Dr. Newton reveled in his political connections. It would have been inexpedient for him to take a position that the 1954 Brown v. Board of Education decision was the law of the land.

I never met Dr. Newton. I do not presume to judge his relationship with his God. I have no way of knowing what prodding he may or may not have given privately to his political friends. I prefer to take him at his word in his comment to the newspaper in 1956 about the efforts good Christian people were making in less public ways. His very public position in 1956 at the Georgia Baptist Convention, his pictorially captured political connections and his statements about the Ministers Manifesto are a matter of public record.

CHAPTER 6
OASIS

The Ministers Manifesto of 1957 laid out six principles that guided their thought. Number 3 is as follows:

3. THE PUBLIC school system must not be destroyed. It is an institution essential to the preservation and development of our democracy. To sacrifice that system in order to avoid obedience to the decree of the Supreme Court would be to inflict tremendous loss upon multitudes of children, whose whole lives would be impoverished as a result of such action. It would also mean the economic, intellectual and cultural impoverishment of our section, and would be a blow to the welfare of our nation as a whole.

Since 1955, state law in Georgia had required that funds be cut off from any school system which attempted to integrate – even if in obedience to a federal court order. The eighty signers of the manifesto were staking out a position in direct opposition to state law. In January of 1958, just two months after the manifesto was published, a group of Atlanta Negroes filed a class action suit in federal court, (Calhoun et al vs. Latimer), against the Atlanta School Board. The suit asked that the School Board be enjoined from practicing racial discrimination in the public schools (Background Atlanta, 1961, p.6). Almost four years after the initial Brown vs. Board of Education decision, the issue was now joined in Georgia.

It seemed inevitable that Atlanta schools would be ordered to desegregate. This would put Atlanta on a collision course with state law, which would require that schools in the district be closed. On December 9, 1958, eighteen white Atlanta parents formed HOPE (Help Our Public Schools) (Background Atlanta, 1961). Their position was simple – keep public schools open. Period. HOPE was opposed by well-organized and well-funded organizations such as the States Rights Council, the Ku Klux Klan, the White Citizens Council and MASE (Metropolitan Association for Segregated Education).

In June of 1959, U.S. District Judge Frank Hooper ruled in favor of the plaintiffs. The Atlanta School Board was ordered to submit a plan for desegregation by December of that year. On November 30th, the Atlanta School Board submitted a plan wherein students could make application to attend schools of their choice, beginning with the 12th grade and expanding to each lower grade in successive years. Judge Hooper approved the plan on January 20, 1960 and ordered it into effect in September. The Georgia General Assembly would, however, need to enact statutes to allow the schools to remain open.

Initially, the General Assembly authorized a commission to hold public meetings in each of Georgia's ten congressional districts. The commission consisted of nineteen members and was chaired by John Sibley. The seventy-one year old Sibley had been a judge in Milledgeville and had served as general counsel of the Coca-Cola Co. At the time, he was president of Trust Company Bank (Larrabee, 2004). The "General Assembly Committee on Schools" became known as the Sibley Commission.

A group of ministers, including my father, called on Mr. Sibley in his office at Trust Company Bank. Their purpose was to encourage open schools. Mr. Sibley recognized that the congregations of these pastors were not, themselves, integrated. He wanted to know why they were pushing for open schools when their own churches were not open. The answer, as addressed in Chapter 5, was that the churches were not dictatorships. Many times, those decisions were made by a board regardless of the minister's position on the subject.

One of the public meetings authorized by the Sibley Commission was held at Southwest High School in Atlanta. My older sister, Karen, attended that school, as would I upon entering in 1962. My father was in attendance at this meeting as was Lester Maddox. As was the custom in the Deep South at the time, the meeting was closed with a prayer, which my father was asked to deliver. Maddox, probably sensing that the majority sentiment was in favor of open schools, attempted to shout down my father during the prayer. He continued to rant as Dad prayed on. When Karen arrived at school the next day, there was quite a buzz about the "confrontation" between Dad and Lester Maddox. Maddox, as will be seen in Chapter 9, was quite the folk hero among segregationists in Georgia.

The committee issued its report in April of 1960. By a vote of 11 to 8, the committee recommended a Freedom of Choice Plan (Background Atlanta, 1961). The voters of each school district would be allowed to determine whether their schools would remain open. The legislative session of the Georgia General Assembly had ended prior to the committee's report. Judge Hooper realized that if the Atlanta School District integrated in September, per his order, state law would require that the schools be closed. He issued a stay of his order to September of 1961. In January of 1961, the Georgia General Assembly repealed the mandatory closing laws.

The Atlanta School Board had devised a plan under which African-American students would make application to attend previously white schools. Applications were received from 133 students between May 1st and May 15th. Ten applications were approved to attend 11th or 12th grades at four high schools. One of those schools, Brown High School, was in West End. Many of the youth in our church attended Brown, which was the main rival in sports to Southwest.

Although the number was small, black students would be attending school with whites with the opening of schools in the fall. Members of the Open School Movement began focusing their attention on "calm, dignified compliance with the law" (Background Atlanta, 1961, p.13). Atlanta did not want a repeat of Little Rock.

Out of the desire for a peaceful desegregation of the schools, sprang a group called OASIS, comprised of 53 affiliate organizations. The name OASIS was an acronym for Organizations Assisting Schools in September. The Atlanta Regional Consortium for Higher Education, in its 2004 publication <u>Atlanta in the Civil Rights Movement,</u>

cites OASIS as being a "biracial coalition" as opposed to other groups in the Open Schools movement, such as the NAACP and HOPE. This biracial cooperation was born out of the ongoing meetings which resulted from the 1957 Ministers' Manifesto.

The primary purpose of OASIS was to use existing organizational structures to encourage peaceful compliance on the day of school desegregation. The affiliates of OASIS were divided into three sections: Religious, Civic and Service Groups, and Youth-Serving Agencies. Public meetings were held. A speaker's bureau provided speakers for service groups. A troupe of Theater Atlanta Players presented skits on desegregation to teenagers at youth camps and civic centers.

My father was co-chair of the Religious section of OASIS along with Rev. Nat Long, the pastor of the Druid Hills Methodist Church. Rev. Long had also been one of the original signers of the Ministers' Manifesto. Dad was probably chosen because of his two-year presidency of the Atlanta Christian Council in 1959–1960. On New Year's Day in 2005, my father penned an account of a conversation he had with Bishop Hiland of the Roman Catholic Diosese in which he requested that Bishop Hiland appoint a representative to work with OASIS. Dad told Bishop Hiland that the committee viewed the participation of the Roman Catholic clergy as essential in their efforts.

Bishop Hiland expressed appreciation for the efforts of OASIS, but pointed out that the Roman Catholics had their own schools and were, therefore, not directly affected by the public school desegregation. He also stated that the Roman Catholic Church was a very dogmatic church and did not easily participate in interfaith efforts.

My father responded that his denomination had frequently been accused of being every bit as dogmatic as the Roman Catholic Church. "What denomination might that be?" asked Bishop Hiland. "The Southern Baptist Convention" replied my father. After a long silence, Bishop Hiland continued, "I think we can do business together." He appointed a representative who attended every committee meeting faithfully.

A few days after the conversation, a bus carrying civil rights leaders on a tour of southern cities was attacked in Anniston, AL. My father received a letter from Bishop Hiland stating that the events in Anniston had underscored, for him, the importance of the work of OASIS.

The day of desegregation of the four Atlanta high schools was set for Wednesday, August 30, 1961. The Religious section of OASIS spearheaded the observance of "Law and Order Weekend" (Friday, August 25th through Sunday August 27th). Churches of all denominations and faiths conducted special prayers for a peaceful transition.

The pastors of each church whose services were broadcast on television or radio were asked to close their services on Sunday August 27th with a plea for peaceful behavior on Wednesday. At West End Baptist Church, this required the approval of the deacons. They did give their approval. My father was to broadcast the plea, and the chairman of deacons would follow it with a statement that he was acting with the support of the church and deacon board. So much had changed since November of 1956.

At the close of the deacons' meeting, Jimmy McGarrity approached my father. He asked if Dad remembered his request of years earlier that Dad pray for him. Dad said that, yes, he remembered it. He added that he would like to say that he had prayed every day for Jimmy.

But he could say that he had prayed frequently for him. Jimmy said, "I think it's working, Pastor." Dad responded, "Yes, I think it is."

For one day, Atlanta became the focal point in the desegregation issue. Virginia H. Hein, writing in 1972 in The Image of "A City Too Busy to Hate": Atlanta in the 1960's, wrote:

> The world *did* seem to be watching. As August 30 approached, members of the press and other news media poured into Atlanta, and Atlanta – the city which Ralph McGill said "has always tried to look forward and not backward" – was ready for them. Each one was given the unique handbook, *Background: Atlanta*, prepared by OASIS "for reporters covering the desegregation of Atlanta Public Schools" (Hein, 1972, p.205).

The handbook contained a forward by Ralph McGill along with information on the ten black students and the four high schools. The mayor, William Hartsfield, and the police chief, Herbert Jenkins, wrote letters to the press. There was a factual history of events in Atlanta and Georgia from May of 1954 to present. Most telling, however, was "An Editorial P.S. We Hope You Will Read," written by Mrs. David Neiman, Public Information Chairman of OASIS. In it, one senses the uncertainty of how the events of that Wednesday in August would unfold:

> In writing the foregoing piece, we have tried to give you "just the facts." Now let us tell you what's in our hearts. We had a

double purpose in preparing this kit. If our schools desegregate smoothly and without incident – and the overwhelming majority of Atlantans are praying that they will – we wanted you to know why. If a rock is thrown or a demonstration staged, you ought to know that is not the whole story of our city.

Ask any of our local newsmen to tell you about the "Open Schools Movement." They'll say we're a bunch of starry-eyed amateurs – a strictly grassroots-type operation held together chiefly with scotch tape and imagination. But they'll also tell you that *we held together* – through three interminable uphill years to accomplish what those who thought they knew all about Georgia said never would happen in our generation.

Who took part in the "Open Schools Movement?" The ordinary people who live in Atlanta – and believe it or not, much of Georgia. The printer who donated pamphlets and handbills on a "pay if you get it" basis. The businessmen who gave an office and typewriter, stationary, erasers and all that scotch tape. The lawyers who volunteered their time and brainpower to unsnarl the tangled legal thickets. But most of all, the women of Atlanta who licked the stamps, organized the meetings and stayed on the telephone until they finished the job. Yes, the unsung heroines of the "Open Schools Movement" are mostly ordinary housewives and mothers who left beds unmade and meals uncooked to insure their children's educational future.

Is it over yet? Not by a long shot. There are those with whom old ways die-hard. We have heard the nation's most militant racists are marshaling their forces to make a stand at this "Second Battle of Atlanta." You must have heard it too – or most of you wouldn't be here.

When the "symbolic ten" go to their classrooms, segregation in Georgia's common schools will officially be over. There are those who wish the ten could be a thousand. There are many who object to even one. But whatever the views that divide them, Atlantans are united in a single hope that the story that unfolds on August 30th will be much different from the one you might have expected. And when ten Negro children go to school on Wednesday, the heart of Atlanta will go with them (Background Atlanta, 1961, pp. 14–15).

The events of August 30th were peaceful. President Kennedy held a news conference that evening. The bulk of the news conference covered issues related to foreign affairs and domestic politics. However, he opened the news conference with four announcements. He began with Atlanta:

First, I want to take this opportunity to congratulate Governor Vandiver of Georgia, Mayor Hartsfield of Atlanta, Chief of Police

Jenkins, Superintendent of Schools Letson and all of the parents, students and citizens of Atlanta, Ga. for the responsible, law-abiding manner in which four high schools were desegregated today.

This was the result of vigorous effort for months by the officials of Atlanta and by groups of citizens throughout the community. Their efforts have borne fruit in the orderly manner in which desegregation was carried out – with dignity and without incident.

Too often, in the past, such steps in other cities have been marred by violence and disrespect for the law (Public Papers of John Kennedy, 1961).

Reed Sarratt, in The Ordeal of Desegregation: The First Decade, wrote:

The start of desegregation in September was calm, and OASIS disbanded, its job completed. Within a few weeks the board of directors of HOPE decided to close its office but to be ready on a "standby basis" if needed. Mrs. Benson Downing, chairman, said, "Atlanta had given us a blueprint, and each community must be ready when the time comes to desegregate (Sarratt, 1966, p. 316).

The 1961 desegregation of Atlanta schools was, indeed, symbolic. The pace of desegregation continued to be slow. My first year of high school was the 1962–1963 school year. That would have been the second school year of desegregation. No African-American students attended my school, Southwest High School, that year. However, each year saw an increase in the number of black students allowed to transfer. Though symbolic, the events of August 30, 1961 diffused the tension and anger in Atlanta. The deed was done, and no amount of fighting would undo it. By 1961, the city's golf courses and public transportation were already integrated. Schools represented the last stand. Diehard segregationists shifted their focus to the rights of private establishments to refuse service to anyone of their choosing. That issue was still charged with emotion for both sides, but those battles paled in comparison to the school issue.

The disbanding of OASIS marked the end of Dad's highly public profile. He remained active in the Atlanta Christian Council, but things calmed down significantly. In 1963, we celebrated the tenth anniversary of his pastorate at West End Baptist Church. Dad always felt that he would serve West End for ten years. In June of 1963, he accepted a call from the Calvary Baptist Church of Kansas City, MO. He submitted his resignation to West End Baptist Church on Sunday, June 9, 1963 at the close of the morning worship service. *The Atlanta Constitution* reported the news on the following Tuesday with the following:

> During his 10-year stay here he twice was president of the Atlanta Christian Council and a leader in efforts to prepare for school desegregation in 1961 through OASIS – Organizations Assisting Schools in September.
>
> A recurring theme in his sermons was that Christians cannot "be indifferent to the

law or rebellious to the courts which administer it."

In a sermon in 1959, Dr. Shands called the status of the Negro "an indictment of white Christian men," and said Christians must take the lead in removing "barriers between men."

In Kansas City, Dad continued his lifelong commitment to cooperation and understanding across racial lines. He participated in a joint committee of pastors from the Kansas City Baptist Association and the National Baptist Convention. Our church, Calvary Baptist, participated in a one-time pulpit swap with the Paseo Baptist Church. My father and choir led worship at Paseo Baptist and their pastor, D.A. Holmes, and their choir led worship at Calvary. When Pastor Holmes retired in 1967, Pastor Charles Briscoe became pastor in his place. Pastor Briscoe had been a member of the committee of pastors mentioned above. My father had the honor of preaching his installation sermon.

CHAPTER 7
SOUTHERNER BY BIRTH

T he second paragraph of the Ministers' Manifesto
begs the question, "What does it mean to be a
Southerner?"

The signers of this statement are all ministers
of the Gospel, but we speak also as citizens of
Georgia and of the United States of America.
We are all Southerners, either by birth or by
choice, and speak as men who love the South,
who seek to understand its problems, and who
are vitally concerned for its welfare.

The meeting of the deacons at West End Baptist
Church that was called in 1956 to censure my father began
with John Still saying that he was a Southerner "complete
with all its meanings."

I loved the South. My first concrete memory of the
South was of Robert E. Lee. I decided that I was named for
him. He seemed so much more polished than the pictures I
would see of Northern generals. Lee looked so stately in his

gray uniform. His white beard always appeared trimmed. Sherman and Grant always appeared to have "scraggly" beards, and the northern blue uniform seemed so harsh. Lee's mount, Traveler, was a fine white horse with a dark mane and tale. Everything about Lee seemed grand and stately.

Surely Lee had to have been the finest general of either army. I remembered being told how Lincoln had offered Lee the command of the Army of the Potomac. Lee turned him down out of loyalty to his native Virginia.

I learned about the Mason-Dixon line in when I was in the fourth grade. Wow, there was actually a **border** between the North and the South. Louisville, KY was at the northern end of the South and sat on the Mason-Dixon line. I was familiar with Louisville. My father traveled there often as a trustee of the Southern Baptist Theological Seminary. Louisville seemed pretty far north to me. I had heard my father and mother talk of snow storms in Louisville in their student days in the 1940's. It rarely snowed in Atlanta.

The South had a sense of chivalry and honor. Sherman had marched through the South and burned Atlanta to the ground. Surely, Lee would never have done something that barbaric. To this day, when holding a door open for a lady, I offer the explanation that "I was born in the South." One never stops being a Southern gentleman.

I was fortunate enough to acquire a few Civil War bullets. We lived on Highview Road, the highest spot in Atlanta. The fiercest fighting in the Battle of Atlanta had occurred right here, according to the historian who lived at the foot of the street. My best friend, Greg Pinson, lived across the street. Greg was the second boy I met the first day I lived in Atlanta. There were woods behind Greg's house. Greg's father worked in the hardware industry. On occasion, he would bring a metal detector home from work. Greg and I would comb the woods looking for Civil War artifacts. We found many bullets. Greg got to keep the really neat items, since his Dad had provided the metal detector. We found belt buckles, partial cannon balls and what looked like mess kits. Once we found a Confederate bullet that had collided head on with a Yankee bullet. The heat of the bullets had fused them together. I cringe when I imagine how much lead was flying that day.

Another time, as I cut our front lawn after a hard rain, I saw something barely protruding from the red Georgia clay in a bare spot of our lawn under a large tree. It was a Confederate bullet. The Civil War had ended less than 100 years earlier, and here was a bullet just lying in the ground. Of course, we cherished the Confederate bullets that we found. Yankee bullets were more sharply pointed and had three bands of grooves near the base of the bullet. Confederate bullets were rounder and had two bands of grooves.

Yankees talked funny, or course. But they made fun of the way we talked. When Shake and Bake coating for chicken first hit the markets, there was a television commercial featuring a little girl telling her father "Weyuh havin' frahd chickin tonaht. And Ah hayulped." We all complained about how overstated the accent was. Yankees must have produced the commercial.

There was much talk of the South rising again. Most of it I heard from classmates in school. It didn't seem very plausible to me. I was pretty sure we weren't going to have another war with the North, but there certainly seemed to be a lot of conviction behind the statements.

Imagine my horror at learning I would be moving to the North in 1963 at the age of fourteen. We were moving to Kansas City. I was told that things were done differently up north. Things were going to be more formal. I would be required to wear a coat and tie to evening events that would have required only an open-collar white shirt in Atlanta.

I hated it.

I now was the one who talked funny. I was teased for a penny being a "peonie". A pen was a "peun". Five was "fiii". Had the teasing been strictly from boys, I probably would have kept my accent forever. I lost it in six months.

But the girls were much different, too. I had heard a lot about "Southern belles" and how much more advanced Southern girls were. It was true. The girls my age in Kansas City were not as advanced in dress or makeup usage as twelve year olds in Atlanta. I wouldn't have even looked at twelve-year-old girls in Atlanta. Okay, maybe there was one I can remember. But the difference was striking.

The architecture in Kansas City was just plain ugly to me. There were no houses with columns. There were very few white houses made of siding. Everything seemed to be stucco and stone. The lot on which our house sat was a postage stamp compared to my large front and back yards in Atlanta. Greg Pinson and I had played football in our front yards in Atlanta. In Kansas City, we had to play football in the **street.**

I made a new friend early in my first school year in Kansas City. David Shaw and I had much in common. Both of our fathers were ministers. We both played trumpet in the band. We both were sports fanatics. We were the same age. We had both moved to Kansas City in the summer of 1963. But our most binding commonality was that we had both come from the South.

David was born in Atlanta, but he had moved to Kansas City from Louisville, KY. What had seemed pretty far north to me previously now seemed Southern.

The one thing Kansas City offered that neither Atlanta nor Louisville had was major league baseball. Being sports freaks, we attended many Kansas City Athletics games together. It took years for the losing to dampen our enthusiasm. It was, after all, major league baseball. At some point in each Kansas City Athletics game, between innings, the organist would play "Dixie". David and I would stand at attention and place our hands over our hearts. What a sight we must have been. And how ignorant I was.

I did not realize that the Southern way of life had been built on free labor. I was not totally unaware that slavery had existed. I had seen the slave quarters at the Wren's Nest next to West End Baptist Church. I had known that the Civil War was fought, primarily, over slavery. But I did not understand the economics of the South.

My father remembers only one substantive conversation with his father about racial issues. It occurred about the time my father was sixteen. My grandfather made the statement that education of the black man would be the economic undoing of the South. The reason, he explained, would be the loss of cheap labor. Blacks were still performing much of the work in cotton fields and rice paddies. The loss of the Civil War may have meant the end of slavery, but the labor of blacks was still cheap instead of free.

It causes me great pain to think that my son, Bobby, could be constrained to a life as cheap labor as his great grandfather would have preferred.

I see, now, that the attitude of whites toward blacks in the South was a mixture of hatred and fear. Hatred at the loss of free labor. Hatred because of the loss of the war. Hatred born out of a feeling that the Brown vs. Board of Education decision was persecuting the South. And fear that race riots would occur if blacks in the South ever broke free of the economic and legal straps that bound them.

The argument that white supremacists and segregationists made was that they didn't hate anyone. The Civil War had not been fought over slavery. It had been fought over states' rights. The backlash against the Supreme Court after 1954 was not about hatred of blacks. It was, again, over the right of the individual states to administer their education systems.

I think, deep down, Southern leaders knew that the world would see through their states rights arguments and recognize the hatred. The following editorial appeared in *The Atlanta Constitution* on Monday, March 2, 1953.

Have We Lost Our Common Sense?

In the news Saturday were two stories which well illustrate the predicament of the South.

In Washington unconfirmed reports had it that Sen. Richard B. Russell's Jackson-Jefferson Day speech in North Carolina would not be broadcast nationally by the party because the senator had said in advance he intended to be critical of those in and out of the party who criticize the South for being reactionary, bigoted and narrow.

On the same page was a story in familiar pattern, which illustrates how the South continually is made vulnerable to criticism and why Senator Russell must seek to defend it.

Two Georgia legislators presumably went to see the musical show "South Pacific," which has pleased millions. Yet these two legislators, in a fantastic decision, say they will seek to prevent "South Pacific" from being shown again in Georgia because of the contents of a song.

The song has lines which say one has to be taught to be afraid of people whose eyes are oddly made, of people whose skin is a different shade . . . "You've got to be taught before it's too late . . . to hate all the people your relatives hate."

Senator Russell and other Southerners who seek to have the South turn its best face to the nation will have difficulty getting around this newest example of why the South is vulnerable to criticism.

The story will get nationwide publicity, which may be the reason, although we trust not, why the statements were made. But the point is that Georgia is placed in a ridiculous position.

There are millions who don't think the song means what the two legislators say it does. It is true that one must learn to hate.

Babies aren't born with hate as an instinct. They do pick up hatreds.

For all its banality, the song from "South Pacific" basically states a truth. Surely it is not too late for common sense to direct our actions.

There was nothing about the household in which my father was raised that would have led him to take the positions he took that were so out of the mainstream of Southern life. My grandfather, Otis Norman Shands, Sr., was a hard man. He believed in keeping the Negro poor and uneducated. He would, on occasion, drink too much and hit my grandmother.

Grandfather Shands was a barber. He owned a barbershop in Columbus, GA where my father and mother were born and raised. He, himself, was uneducated, having dropped out of school after the third grade. He went to work in a cotton mill sweeping floors. My father tells of the times my grandfather would send him, at the age of five or six, to fetch something in the back of the house. He was not allowed to turn on a light. My grandfather would then throw a shoe into the darkness. If Dad cried or came back without the required object, he would be punished.

My grandfather also had a temper. He employed a Negro "boy" at his barbershop. He was not a boy at all, but a man named Sherman Caldwell. His duties included sweeping the hair clippings and generally keeping the shop tidy. Every barbershop I can remember in the South employed such a "boy". One day, my grandfather took exception to the manner in which Sherman was sweeping. He snatched the broom from Sherman and began beating him with it around the head and shoulders. He drove

Sherman from the shop with the invective-laden instruction to never return.

My father, about 14 at the time, witnessed the event. Sherman had taken a liking to Dad and treated him kindly. Such treatment of blacks was not uncommon in Columbus, GA in 1930. Dad had seen it before. But this time he was torn between feelings of loyalty to his father and a nagging feeling that this was wrong. It was the first time he had given any thought to the treatment of blacks. Dad was a Southerner and had accepted all of the Southern attitudes toward blacks.

Grandfather Shands died in July of 1933. My father was seventeen years old. Dad had taken a job earlier that year at the Archer Hosiery Mill after his graduation from high school in January. Following an apprenticeship of eighteen months, he became a machine operator. He bought his first automobile, a 1934 Nash LaFayette, at the time of his promotion. He was the man of the house with a widowed mother and two younger sisters at home. College did not appear to be an option.

My grandfather had not been a church-going man. But the family home sat next door to the Eastern Heights Baptist Church. Dad began attending Sunday school around the age of eight. Following his father's death, Dad became a much more serious young man. He began praying for guidance in a career. During a revival service in September of 1936, he felt that he was being called to a career in Christian service.

Eastern Heights Baptist Church played an important role in my father's life. Not only did he experience a call to the ministry there, he also met my mother in that church. Mom's family was very poor. Her father had died in 1928. Mom was the third of four children and was thirteen at the time of his death. The members of Eastern Heights Baptist church provided many of the meals for the family. The meals would be left on the back porch. This was done to save my grandmother the embarrassment of taking a handout. Mom loved to sing and dreamed of a career as a singer. But she could not afford singing lessons and was forced to work in retailing after graduating from high school. She had a beautiful voice. I remember how she loved to sing the hymns of the church. She never needed a hymnal. I think she knew every hymn by heart.

Dad's call to the ministry made college possible. The Georgia Baptist Convention had a fund earmarked to subsidize students who were entering the ministry. Dad enrolled in Mercer University in Macon, GA in the fall of 1937. Mercer is affiliated with the Georgia Baptist Convention. The unsubsidized portion of his tuition was $64.00 per semester. He was responsible for room and board. He earned his meals his freshman year by waiting tables in the athletic dorm.

My parents married June 26, 1938 at the end of his freshman year at Mercer. Dad took his first church, Cross Keys Baptist Church in Macon, at a salary of $60.00 per month. This had been his average weekly pay at the Archer Hosiery mill. The church could not afford a full-time pastor; therefore, they held services every other Sunday (morning and evening) and each Wednesday evening. After one year, Dad convinced the deacon board that the church should hold services every Sunday. The church could only afford to pay $80.00 per month, which my father accepted.

The years at Mercer were lean but good years. Dad was a good student, but prone to procrastination. Mom typed his papers, sometimes late into the night before the paper was due. The typewriter was manual, of course, and copies were made through the use of carbon paper. My brother was born in January of 1940. Dad graduated magna cum laude in the spring of 1941. He received the Algernon Sydney Sullivan Award, which is presented to the graduating student who best exemplifies excellence in character, leadership, service to the community, and a commitment to spiritual values.

After graduation, Dad stayed at Mercer in the capacity of Baptist Student Union director on a part-time basis. It was in this capacity that events occurred that challenged his Southern upbringing and re-shaped his attitude toward minorities.

In January of 1942, the Baptist Student Union sponsored a Christian Focus Week. Guest speakers, about eight to ten, spoke in chapel, led discussions in classes and preached each evening. One of those guests was a minister named Clarence Jordan (pronounced Jerdan in the Georgia way). Jordan had started a farm, a commune really, in Americus, GA. He named it Koinonia Farms after the Greek word for "community". At Koinonia (pronounced coy-no-nee-uh) blacks and whites lived together and shared all possessions. The mission statement was to:

1. Treat all human beings with dignity and justice.
2. Choose love over violence.
3. Share all possessions and live simply.
4. Be stewards of the land and its natural resources. (Koinonia Partners, 2005)

Dad was moved by Jordan's testimony of his spiritual pilgrimage. He made a vow to God that, with His help, he would treat each human being – regardless of race, class, education or culture – with the respect due to a person created in the image of God and for who Christ died.

Koinonia Farms would experience persecution over the years. On January 15, 1957, its roadside market was bombed for the second time. In March of the same year, a watchman at the farm reported that a man in a car opened fire on him. Later in March a rifle shot was fired at a home on the farm for the second time in a week. Clarence Jordan remained committed to continuing operations. However, half of the personnel of the farm were moved to New Jersey for their safety in April.

Koinonia Farms remained open. In 1968, Clarence Jordan and Millard Fuller changed the focus of the organization and also changed the name to Koinonia Partners. The main focus was Partnership Housing. Houses were built utilizing donated labor and materials. Low-income buyers were given twenty year no interest mortgages. The mortgage payments were placed into a fund to build more houses. Clarence Jordan died in 1969, months before the first home was occupied. The partnership built 194 homes from 1969 to 1992 on Koinonia land as well as in Americus and Plains (Koinonia Partners).

Millard Fuller and his wife Linda ran the program after Jordan's death. In 1976, after three years in Africa, they returned to Americus and formed Habitat for Humanity International.

There was no way of knowing in 1942, at the time Dad made his vow, the extent to which his career would be shaped by this commitment. It would not take long, however, for him to realize that he did, indeed, need God's help in the process of changing his heart and attitudes. My father began his graduate studies at Southern Baptist Seminary in Louisville, KY in September of that year. My mother, father and brother moved into married student housing on campus.

Louisville's proximity to the North meant that not all of the norms and mores of the Deep South were observed. Blacks were not relegated to the back of the bus. Early in 1943, an African-American laborer took a seat next to my father on a bus. My father experienced a classically Southern reaction. His stomach churned and his pulse quickened. He realized that this was the result of his Southern upbringing. He again asked for God's help in dealing with his attitude.

After graduation from the seminary, Dad entered the Navy as a chaplain. He was stationed aboard the aircraft carrier U.S.S. Sadie. While on two weeks of field duty at the Naval Training School in Bainbridge, MD, he counseled an African-American Boatswain's Mate First Class who felt the white sailors were mistreating him. This sailor told my father that he was the first white man who had made him feel like a man instead of a **black** man. This was the first indication my father had that he was making progress in keeping his vow.

Many of my friends who were raised in the North have expressed amazement that Southern attitudes were this strong. Many also have been skeptical of tales of violence directed toward blacks in the South. Again, I point to John Still's opening comments in the Deacon Board meeting of 1956 in which he said he had witnessed, in his youth, the lynching of a black man. The reality is that no jury in the South would convict a white man for killing a black even if a District Attorney would press charges – which was unlikely.

Martin Luther King, Sr. tells of witnessing the beating death of a black man whose only sin was counting his money on payday while walking home from his job at a lumber mill. A belt was tied around his neck, and he was left hanging from a tree (King, 1980).

Emmett Till was beaten to death in Mississippi at the age of fourteen for having whistled at a white woman. A white jury acquitted his killers who later confessed to the murder in a *Look Magazine* interview (*Time*, 2004).

Stetson Kennedy witnessed the beating of a black cab driver whose transgression was picking up white female fares. The man was then forced to run in front of a car full of Klansmen while bullets were fired at his heels. The man stumbled, and the car ran over him, crushing him to death. The next day, the newspaper reported that the man had been found – the apparent victim of a hit and run incident. Kennedy, who had infiltrated the Klan as an informant, relayed the details of the incident to Dan Duke, the Assistant Attorney General of the state of Georgia. Duke articulated the difficulty, if not impossibility, of prosecuting the killers in Kennedy's book The Klan Unmasked:

> "Rockledge County", he said bitterly. "First, I'd play hell getting the prosecutor to issue warrants. Then, if we ever got the case to court, every Ku Kluxer you named would trot a dozen of his lying Brothers across the stand to perjure themselves by swearing he was somewhere else that night. The judge would be against us, and I doubt we could scrape together a jury without at least one Kluxer on it to hang the jury and cause a mistrial. The killers would go free – and your days of usefulness inside the Klan would be over!" (Kennedy, 1990, p. 112).

It is easy for me to understand why some pushed for a law that would make it a federal crime to lynch a black. It is easier to understand why the Southern senators would have fought such a bill. Friends had asked me why such a bill was necessary. Murder was already against the law. The problem lay in getting a county prosecutor to press charges. And, as shown in chapter 2, many considered killing a black as no more consequential than killing a dog. It took the United States Senate until 2005 to publicly apologize for its years of failure to pass anti-lynching legislation.

I realize that being raised a Southern male made an impact on me. As I stated earlier, I had a fierce pride in being a Southerner. My father made a valiant effort to instill Christian values in me. I knew what was accepted at home, but I also was subjected to peer pressure. One day, when I was in sixth or seventh grade, I came home from school having drawn a swastika on the back of my left hand. My father exploded when he saw it during dinner. This was the angriest I had ever seen him. I explained that I only did it because all of the other guys had done it. I didn't know the meaning of it. He told me in no uncertain terms that it was a symbol of hate and I was **NEVER** to bring that symbol into our home again. But while I didn't know what a swastika was, I **did** know what a n_____ was. And I heard the lore at school, at baseball practice, and at football practice. Stories were constantly told about n_____s doing horrible things to white children and women. The result was that I developed a fear of blacks.

None of my personal experience with blacks would have led to fear. We had an African-American maid in Spartanburg, SC where I was born. She was a constant companion until we moved to Gaffney, SC when I was three years old. I have very vague memories of Bell. When we would visit Spartanburg after having moved away, we would visit Bell at her house. She was a kindly woman. She was the first black person with whom my mother ever had consistent contact. Mom attributed some of her vast cooking skills to Bell – particularly the ability to cook cabbage without burning it. My sister Karen, who is 3 ½ years older than I, has very fond memories of Bell. She was part of the family. My parents always encouraged Bell to take her lunch with them at the dining table instead of eating alone in the kitchen, as was expected of maids. Bell declined for some time but finally relented with the stipulation that the drapes be drawn. There could be repercussions for her or our family if others witnessed it.

In Atlanta, we also had a maid. We shared her services with another family. She was also a kind and helpful woman. On rainy days, my mother would give her a ride to and from the bus stop at the end of our street. She was very appreciative. But, in spite of my only personal experiences being positive, society had instilled a fear in me. And fear is the perfect soil in which seeds of hate can flourish.

One of the great ironies of my life is that there was an African-American neighborhood within walking distance of my home. Herring Road was, as I was told, the oldest street in Atlanta. It was the next street over from my street, Highview Road. In fact, the homes across the street and a few houses west backed up to homes on Herring Road. For all of the hysteria that would have occurred had a black moved into any neighborhood in my school district, we were actually neighbors with blacks. I can remember no "incidents" that occurred because of strife in the neighborhood.

But I still had the fear. There was a small shopping district within walking distance of my home. Its name is Cascade Heights. For a young boy, it was the closest thing to heaven imaginable. There was the grocery store, of course. But, more importantly, two drug stores and a dime store. Greg and I were tremendous baseball fans from the age of seven. The dime store offered the lure of baseball cards and the awful cardboard tasting bubble gum in each pack. We usually took the longer route, down Beecher Rd., in walking to Cascade Heights. But the short cut was down Herring Road. And I can remember the fear.

The homes on Herring Road were understandably older and smaller than my house. I never walked down Herring Road without the gripping fear that I would be descended upon by hordes of blacks in retribution for walking in their neighborhood.

Once, as Greg and I were walking down Herring Road, a black woman approached us walking in the other direction. Greg greeted her, "Hi Fannie." I was mortified and absolutely frightened to death. I thought he was using Fannie as a universal moniker for a black woman. I'm sure that was because of "Aunt Fannie's Cabin", one of Atlanta's more popular restaurants at the time. It turns out that Fannie was his family's maid. He had a good laugh for years over my panic, and all was well.

Another time my family was driving across town on a late on a Saturday afternoon to visit my Aunt Dorothy and my cousins. We drove through what would be considered the slums. Of course, it was called N_____ Town. I would never have referred to it that way in front of my father. But that was how I referred to it around my friends. There I was, safe in the back seat of the 1956 Buick with Mom and Dad in the front seat. And I was afraid.

It is precisely because of this fear that I know I could have been fertile ground for prejudiced and bigoted ideas. In fact, some forms of bigotry did manifest themselves in my actions. I love jokes. And I love telling jokes. I have pictures of myself poolside at a convention in 1980 holding court in the midst of about ten people as I told joke after joke. Many of the jokes I told were blatantly prejudicial and demeaning of blacks. I would usually preface the jokes by saying "I'm not prejudiced, but it's **JUST A JOKE.** I thought the jokes were just too funny to not be told. I finally culled such jokes from my repertoire around the age of forty. I am ashamed that it took me that long.

I am aware, however, that I assimilated my father's attitudes toward social justice much more rapidly – and at a much earlier age – than I did the teachings of the Christian faith. Much of my religious education came through rote memory and osmosis. I knew what I was *supposed* to believe, but it was not *mine* until much later in life. Not until I had been knocked to my knees by the experiences of life. But, in the area of civil rights, my father found a way to frame the issue in ways that became personal to me at a very early age. Because of this, even though I will always consider myself a Southerner, the attitudes of the South never fully took root.

CHAPTER 8
THE ICE CREAM CONE

It was one of life's truly mundane car rides. A trip to Cascade Heights to the barbershop. I'm sure that's where Dad was taking me for it was rare for us to be in the car alone going anywhere else. We were almost to the barbershop on the corner of Beecher Rd and Sewell Road when Dad related a conversation to me that would impact me all my life.

A friend of Dad's had told him about the most difficult moment of his life. His son had seen some boys coming out of a neighborhood drug store with ice cream cones. His son also wanted an ice cream cone. This man had to tell his son that he, unlike the other boys, couldn't have an ice cream cone. Hurt and confused, the son wanted to know why. "Because we're black" was the answer.

That moment was branded into the tissue of my brain. I remember the direction the car was headed. I remember that we were directly across from the Beecher Hills Baptist Church. Dad had framed the racial issue in a way that I could understand. I couldn't relate to the father's emotions. But I could sure relate to wanting an ice cream cone and being told I couldn't have one while other boys could. I was about eight years old, and I loved ice cream cones from the drug store.

The boy was Martin Luther King, Jr.

The father was Martin Luther King, Sr.

My father had known Martin Sr. virtually since our arrival in Atlanta. Dad had been asked to participate on a committee of the Atlanta Baptist Association. This committee held regular meetings with members of the National Baptist Convention in Atlanta. Dr. King, Sr. was a representative of the National Baptist Convention at those meetings.

At one meeting, Dad and Dr. William Holmes Borders, pastor of the Wheat Street Baptist Church, were asked to speak to the group. Dr. Borders was arrested in 1957, along with five other African-American ministers, for attempting to sit in the "whites only" section of a city bus. When it was my father's turn to speak at the meeting, he told the story of the Pentecostal minister who had visited West End Baptist Church in 1954.

Years later, Dr. King, Sr. asked to speak to a different group of white ministers to express concerns about racial issues in churches. Dr. King and his wife had attempted to worship at the First Baptist Church of Atlanta and were led to an overflow room equipped with closed circuit televisions while seats remained available in the main sanctuary. The excuse was that those seats were being held for church members who were in Sunday school and who would arrive momentarily. Rather than accept this slight, Dr. King and his wife left. It was this event that caused Dr. King to request a meeting with the ministers group. In his

116

address, Dr. King referred to Dad's earlier remarks to the joint ministers group. He said that, until hearing the story of the Pentecostal minister, he had assumed that the pastors of white churches had not attempted to lead their congregations in opening their church doors or on racial issues in general. Upon hearing Dad, he gained an appreciation of the difficulties white pastors faced, particularly in Southern Baptist churches. Dr. King had assumed that white congregations followed the leadership of the pastor in the same manner of African-American congregations.

Because of this relationship between Dr. King, Sr. and my father, I almost attended the funeral of Martin Luther King, Jr.

I was a freshman at the University of Kansas in April 1968. Spring break was days away when Dr. King, Jr. was assassinated on April 4th. My mother and I were planning to drive to Atlanta and were to be in the city on the day for which the funeral was planned. Dad called Daddy King, as he was affectionately known, and explained that he would not be able to return to Atlanta for the funeral. He said that I would be in town and would attend as his representative. I was very impressed that my father could pick up the phone and reach Daddy King at such a time. It is only in the writing of this book that I have come to appreciate all that went into forming the relationship that resulted in that phone call.

Unfortunately, for me, 1968 was an election year. Party conventions had not yet been held in April; therefore, there were still many candidates. Of course, all of them announced that they would attend the funeral. President Johnson did not attend, but sent Hubert Humphrey. My memory is that Edmund Muskie, Bobby Kennedy, George Romney, and Richard Nixon would all be in attendance.

Dad decided that there would be a circus atmosphere at the funeral. He called Daddy King back and told him that he didn't want him to have to look out for me in those circumstances. I would not attend the funeral.

I was offended. I was nineteen years old and, in my mind, needed no one to "look out for me." My protests went unheeded.

On the morning of the funeral, Mom and I were to drive from Atlanta to Columbus, GA. We were on an overpass above Auburn Ave. as the caisson carrying Dr. King's body passed underneath.

My father had more contact on a continuing basis with Dr. King, Sr. than with Martin Luther King, Jr. He did, however, serve on many panel discussions with him during the school desegregation deliberations. At one point, Dad attempted to arrange for MLK, Jr. to preach at West End Baptist Church. He and a deacon attended a sermon preached by Dr. King, Jr. The deacon was disappointed in Dr. King's preaching style. He was expecting a fiery political speech instead of a thoughtful sermon. He would not be in favor of an invitation to Dr. King to preach at our church. Other deacons complained that Dr. King was always speaking of civil disobedience. My father thought, to himself, how fortunate Atlanta was that this was the course Dr. King had chosen.

Martin Luther King, Jr. was a national figure. To many, he was a racial agitator, a troublemaker, and a communist. He seemed more personal to us. He lived in Atlanta. He, his father, and other civil rights leaders were everyday people about whom my father talked around the dinner table as he recounted the activities of his daily life and issues with which he was dealing.

It was at that dinner table that a second event occurred that framed the civil rights struggle for me in very personal terms.

Vacation Bible School. What an oxymoron. How are you on vacation if you have to go to school? That was always how I approached VBS, as it was called. It seems as if it always fell the second week after school let out for the summer. I had just gotten out of school, and now I had to go to church school for half a day for ten days to two weeks.

There was, however, one thing I like about VBS. My father would come home for lunch. Sometimes we would even fire up the grill and cook hamburgers.

On one of those early summer days in approximately 1960, we were having lunch in the breakfast room. We had just arrived home from VBS. My father was reading the mail as my mother finished getting lunch on the table. I sat at the foot of the table, and my father sat at the head.

My father was crying! Just the watery, red eyed, runny nose kind of crying. But I don't believe I had ever seen my father cry.

I asked my father what was wrong. My juvenile reasoning told me that someone surely had died. My father responded that he was reading a letter from a Nigerian student named Deji Adejojin.

Deji was coming to Atlanta to attend Morehouse College. Our church was going to help provide living expenses for Deji. At the urging of Scott Patterson, a retired missionary to Nigeria, the church had previously provided living expenses for another Nigerian student, Theophilus Adejunmobe, to attend the Southern Baptist Theological Seminary in Louisville. After he returned to Nigeria, Adejunmobe wrote an article for a Baptist newspaper about his experiences. Deji had read the article and written to the church to ask for similar support.

In the letter Dad was reading, Deji professed his gratitude to the church. And his letter brimmed with anticipation of worshipping with his brothers and sisters in Christ – people who would do such a thing for him.

My father explained to me that he would have to somehow find a way to tell Deji that he would not be welcome in our church. I cannot imagine the heartache my father felt. I know from conversations with him that he wrestled with this during the weeks before the beginning of the fall semester. On Deji's first day at Morehouse, Dad delivered some bedding and personal supplies to him. Dad explained the situation and offered to introduce Deji to the pastor of a church near the Morehouse campus.

Deji sought to relieve Dad's pain by telling him of the prejudice that produced conflict between the Yoruba and Ibo tribes in Nigeria. Deji believed that the only answer to prejudice was the change Jesus Christ brings to the human heart.

My father invited Deji to speak to the church on the last Sunday night in December. That day was known as Student Night at Christmas in the Southern Baptist denominational calendar. He suggested that Deji thank the church for its help and tell of Baptist mission work in Nigeria. He suggested that Deji wear his Nigerian robe. Some of the church members exited the sanctuary through side or back doors to avoid shaking hands with Deji. Dad was embarrassed. As Dad drove Deji home that evening, Deji commented on the beauty of the sanctuary and the wonderful nature of the people. Dad asked Deji how he could make that comment about the people. Deji responded by telling Dad of a fellow student from Kenya whose faith had been shaken by the prejudice he experienced in Atlanta. Deji said he had told his friend that he was discouraged because his eyes were on men. He should focus on Jesus Christ in whom he could always trust. Such maturity for a young man in his twenties.

Deji was a guest in our house on at least one occasion. I remember that he always had a smile on his face. And, of course, I remember his Nigerian accent. My friend Greg Pinson came to the front door to ask me to play baseball while Deji was there. Deji asked us if we liked "beezbol". I think Greg and I always referred to baseball as beezbol after that.

My sister Karen is three years older than I. She was a junior or senior in high school when Deji visited our home. One of her classmates came to the house to pick up some school notes from Karen. He saw Deji from the front door and refused to enter the house. The next day, the school was buzzing over Karen's "n_____ boyfriend."

I would hear of Deji often from my father. Deji became an executive with Mobil Oil in Nigeria. His work would bring him to the United States for conferences. He would always call Dad. He sent many gifts of Nigerian art to our family.

Deji was bright, good natured and articulate. He had faith that could move mountains. My exposure to Deji made it impossible for me to accept the inferiority of another person simply based on skin color.

CHAPTER 9
RACISM'S FACE

In My Father's House

I n my mind's eye, racism had a face in Atlanta in the 50's and early 60's. That face was the face of Lester Maddox.

Racism had many names: Marvin Griffin, Herman Talmadge, Ernest Vandiver, Richard Russell. But it had one face: Lester Maddox.

Maddox owned a restaurant, the Pickrick, on Highway 41 near the campus of Georgia Tech. His specialty was skillet-fried chicken. This was the way my mother fried chicken – in a skillet. The food was served cafeteria style. The clientele included blue-collar families and college students. Blacks were not allowed, but that was common of all restaurants and lunch counters in Atlanta.

But the Pickrick was different from most other restaurants and lunch counters. Maddox ran an advertisement in the Saturday editions of *The Atlanta Constitution* and *The Atlanta Journal* that was more political column than advertising. In it he regaled against local government and the Atlanta newspapers and expressed his political views.

Maddox ran his first ad on Saturday, October 28, 1950. Bob Short, in his biography of Maddox titled <u>Everything is Pickrick</u>, gives the following analysis of Maddox's advertisements:

> By September of 1954, Maddox's folksy tone and chatty, homespun wisdom began to win him a faithful following. Not only were the ads causing the Pickrick to grow by leaps and bounds, but Lester was becoming something of a local celebrity. During the spring of 1955, a photograph of a balding, bespectacled Maddox with an impish grin was added alongside the "Pickrick Says" banner. With the addition, the advertisements took on the look of an op-ed piece on the editorial page. It was a political column posing as a restaurant ad. Along with the new look, political themes – comments about city taxes, possible candidates for the next county commission seats as well (as) questions as to why a highway had not been completed – started seeping into the copy (Short, 1999, p.35)

Lester Maddox – The first blogger.

At one point, the *Constitution* and the *Journal* told Maddox they would no longer accept his advertisements due to the insightful nature of his comments. They relented after Maddox took his ads to smaller local papers and ran them under the heading "The Atlanta Newspapers refused to run this ad." The Saturday editions of the paper had become popular as people purchased them to see what Maddox would say next and about whom he would say it. Circulation suffered when they pulled his ads.

Maddox, in his autobiography <u>Speaking Out: The Autobiography of Lester Garfield Maddox,</u> refers to his difficulties with the Atlanta newspapers:

> The Cox Atlanta newspaper monopoly, The *Constitution* and the *Journal,* were adamantly opposed to my conservative and segregationist philosophy, and I found myself continually running into obstacles from the people I had to buy my advertising space from (Maddox, 1975, p. 30).

The editor of *The Atlanta Constitution* was named Ralph McGill. He took editorial positions championing the plight of the Negro. This earned him Maddox's contempt. Atlanta's mayor, William B. Hartsfield, had been in office all but 18 months since 1936. Maddox believed that a corrupt political machine ran Atlanta.

There were, therefore, recurring themes in the "Pickrick Says" ads: segregation, city government and the Atlanta newspapers. And anyone who didn't agree with Maddox was a communist. Many letters to the editor referred to the hatefulness of Maddox's diatribes. Maddox always responded that he didn't hate anyone. He wasn't against anything. He was **for** God, country and the constitution of the United States. His view was that the targets of his animosity were against those things.

In the Democratic primary election for mayor of Atlanta in 1957, Maddox supported a close friend, Archie Lindsay, in a race against Hartsfield. Lindsay was a county commissioner, a Sunday school teacher in Lester's Southern Baptist church and a frequent customer of the Pickrick. Lindsay was defeated in the primary by a slim margin of 3804 votes.

On July 18, 1954, Maddox announced his candidacy as an independent in the general election on December 4th. Maddox needed to acquire roughly 4500 signatures on a petition in order to get his name on the ballot. He obtained twice that number.

Maddox was the true outsider running against the entrenched political machine. The number of votes cast in the election was 65,287. Prior to this, the highest number of votes on record in an Atlanta general election had been 10,000. Hartsfield received 63% of the vote. Maddox received only 37%, but with 23,987 votes, he certainly learned that he had achieved name recognition.

The mayoral election of 1957 is my earliest memory of Lester Maddox. I knew that my father voted for Hartsfield. In December 1957, I was a little more than one month shy of my 9th birthday. I had become aware of politics by watching the 1956 Democratic National Convention. My father was, and is to this day, a staunch Democrat. I knew that he supported Adlai Stevenson. My first memory of the convention was the band playing "Happy Days Are Here Again" when Estes Kefauver, from our neighboring state of Tennessee, was nominated as Vice President on Democratic ticket. I was becoming aware of politics. My parents were avid readers of the newspaper. I became aware of Atlanta politics by listening to them as they discussed events while reading the paper.

Example of a Pickrick Ad
from Lester Maddox.
The Atlanta Constitution,
June 15, 1963

My take on Maddox was that he was a joke. He was a mousy looking, bald man with glasses and, by his own description, "jug ears". He did not look "political" whatever that means.

Maddox was the antithesis of my father. They were roughly the same age. Maddox was born in 1915 – one year before my father. Both were teenagers during the Depression. Both came from blue-collar backgrounds. The similarities stop there. Maddox dropped out of school in the tenth grade. Many of his opponents used "high school dropout" as an insult. By all accounts, Maddox was industrious and honest. There is no shame, in my mind, in dropping out of school during the Depression. But the bare facts are that my father was an articulate, well-educated man and Lester Maddox was not. I'm sure this registered in my psyche as I evaluated the positions each man took.

In 1961, Maddox decided to make another run for mayor of Atlanta. Hartsfield had decided, at the age of 72, that he would not seek re-election. This time Maddox decided to enter the Democratic primary. The Republican Party was virtually non-existent in the South during these years. It was probably political suicide to enter a race as a Republican with the animosity Eisenhower created by sending the National Guard into Little Rock to force desegregation of the schools.

The Democratic primary took place on September 13, 1961. This was just two weeks after the peaceful desegregation of the Atlanta schools was. 101,000 votes were cast in the primary. Ivan Allen, Jr., the second-generation owner of a successful office supply chain, was the leading vote getter. He received 39,000 votes. Maddox received 21,000 votes. A run-off was required since neither candidate received a majority of the votes.

In the run-off, Allen received 64,313 votes to 36,091 for Maddox. For all of his celebrity and "folk hero" status, Maddox's percentage actually slipped from 37% in 1957 to 36% in 1961.

Maddox was undeterred by his lack of political success. I believe Maddox lived in a self-contained world in which his customer base was constantly supporting him. The restaurant business is a seven-day a week, twelve hour per day venture. Maddox had cultivated a loyal following. Many of them probably ate at the Pickrick as much out of support for Maddox's segregationist views as for the fried chicken. He was probably constantly hearing "attaboys" from most people with whom he came in contact each and every day. This would lead to a heightened, and false, sense of importance.

In any event, Maddox decided to run for Lieutenant Governor in 1962. Again, he came in second in the primary but forced a run-off. Again, he lost. But he garnered 45% of the vote this time. And 181,695 people statewide had voted for him. His opponent, Peter Zack Geer, was also a segregationist.

In the middle of the Lieutenant Governor's race, blacks picketed the Pickrick for the first time. The NAACP was convening their annual convention in Atlanta. On July 3, 1962, some fifty demonstrators from the convention demonstrated outside of the Pickrick. The next day, Maddox sent a telegram to the convention thanking them for the pickets. He noted that the pickets had not only increased his business, but also increased his vote total in the lieutenant governor's race by 50,000 votes (Short, 1999).

The first actual attempt to integrate the Pickrick occurred on May 18, 1963. Four African-Americans and three white demonstrators walked into the Pickrick and took

131

seats. Maddox managed to forcibly move one demonstrator to the door and had an African-American employee forcibly remove another. The remaining demonstrators left of their own accord.

It was not long after this incident that my father resigned his pastorate at West End Baptist Church. Maddox reacted immediately. In his Pickrick "advertisement" the following Saturday, he wrote:

> Three of the really Big Wheels involved in getting up the famous "Ministers Manifesto" several years back have been "Called" out of Atlanta and it looks as though another is on shaky ground and may be "called" any time. If we could do the same with a publisher, an editor, and about three or four columnists, we would be in real good shape.

God and country were recurring themes in Maddox's ads. He was an active member of the North Atlanta Baptist Church. His mocking use of the pastoral calling reeks of hypocrisy, in my opinion. In the same "advertisement" Maddox offered up the following tidbits:

> A great tragedy of our time is that public officials seeking votes, and business leaders seeking dollars, would use and misuse our negro citizens for their own selfish gains. They are nothing but renegades and scalawags and _____. To gain the negro votes and dollars, they are leading him to believe that his race cannot be successful unless integrated into the white race. Every picket at a motel,

hotel, restaurant, cafeteria, etc. is killing any real opportunity for the negro race, by making him, without truth and fact, admit that over twenty million American negroes cannot build their own fine restaurants, cafeteria, motels, hotels, etc. It is deceit by white renegades, who under the pretense of helping our negro citizens are destroying individualism and racial pride while in truth enslaving our negro citizens."

We close with this. After this week, any negro who wants a free ride and fails to support the present President is a fool. Any white man, whether in labor, business, the professions, government or elsewhere, unless he is shiftless and has a free ride, is an even bigger fool if he does support the present President. If we can count our fools, it will be easy to predict our future. Plus racial integrity is one of the high qualities of character for any race. A sensible man of principle, character, care and courage will fight to the death for survival of his race and will not stand for mongrelization of the white and negro races. Surrender to the Communist-inspired (and supported) race mixers means the destruction of both races and the nation. Will you take a stand and admit the preceding statement is true, or will you give it the lie and join the mongrelizers?"

Maddox always claimed that he was not a racist and had no hatred in his heart for anyone. He was only a

segregationist. For my taste, there is enough hatred in this one "advertisement" to show Maddox for what he truly was. A racist hatemonger.

On July 2, 1964, President Johnson signed the Civil Rights Act into law. The next day, three African-American ministers showed up at the Pickrick at 5:30 p.m. Maddox closed the Pickrick each day after the lunch hour and reopened for dinner. The ministers had arrived earlier in the day, only to be told that Maddox would return around 5:30. During the intervening hours, the press had been alerted to the ministers' intentions, as had many Pickrick customers. The press and pick-handle-wielding Pickrick customers were waiting for the confrontation. Maddox described the events in his autobiography:

> The car pulled to a stop and the driver opened his door to get out. But I slammed the door. "You're not getting out here."
>
> The one sitting opposite him opened his door and climbed out, and started around the car.
>
> "You might as well get back in there!" I told him. "You're not going to eat at the Pickrick today or any other time! This is my property, my business, and the Constitution guarantees me the right to operate it my way."
>
> He continued to come around toward our side. Having seen what happened at Leb's, and not knowing what he had in mind, I drew the revolver and ordered him to get off my property.

"Get out of here now," I said. "I have the right to protect my property and myself, and that's what I'll do!"

He looked at me, at the gun in my hand, and he turned around and got back into the car. All around us cameras were clicking and grinding away, and as the car began to pull away a cheer went up from my patrons who had come outside to see what was going on.

The photographs of Lester Maddox and his son, armed with pistol and pick handle in defense of what was theirs, were widely circulated, and everywhere the liberal press made me out a racist and bigot and rabble-rouser. I knew then, just as I know now, that I was trying to protect not only the rights of Lester Maddox, but of every citizen, including the three men I chased off my property, for if they could violate my right of private property, then there would be nothing to prevent me from violating theirs (Maddox, 1975, p. 57).

As the car pulled away, one customer struck the hood of the car with a pick handle while other poked at the ministers through the open car windows.

The scene garnered national attention. Maddox was now famous, not only in Georgia but also the nation. During the days after the incident, the Pickrick's parking lot was full. My father, by now in Kansas City, was not surprised by Maddox's actions.

The blacks that had been denied service filed two actions against Maddox. One, in state court, for pointing the pistol. The second, in federal court, for violating their civil rights. The Justice Department, headed by Attorney General Bobby Kennedy, came down forcefully against Maddox. On July 17, 1964, an injunction was entered against Maddox enjoining him from refusing service to African-Americans. The injunction was to take effect on August 11, 1964.

That day arrived along with more African-Americans demanding service. Maddox prided himself on the fact that he employed forty-five blacks among his roughly 65 employees. Maddox called upon one, Ozell Rogers, to plead with the demonstrators to leave. Rogers was pleading for his job, as Maddox had threatened to close the Pickrick rather than integrate. The demonstrators refused, but the combination of physical restraint by Pickrick customers and a summer shower dispersed the crowd.

Two days later, a federal judge issued an order that Maddox show why he shouldn't be held in contempt of court. A hearing was set for August 20th. That same day, August 13, 1964, two African-Americans, accompanied by two FBI agents, attempted to be served at the Pickrick. Maddox gives the following account:

> This was it. I blocked their way, and looking at the two agitators, I said, "You sorry, no good Communists. You have just put sixty-six people out of work. You've stolen my business. The Pickrick is closed. Now get out of here!" (Maddox, 1975, p.65).

An hour later, Maddox set up a podium outside of the Pickrick. He made an announcement in front of eighty supporters as told by Bob Short:

> "My president, my congress, and the Communists have closed my business and ended a childhood dream," Maddox said, tears streaming down his face. "They have killed my business and helped kill the American free enterprise system" (Short, 1999, p.62).

To his credit, Maddox kept his employees on the payroll for forty-five days. He attempted to make money by selling souvenirs at a stand in the Pickrick's parking lot. Chief among the souvenirs were "Pickrick drumsticks." These were pick handles painted red. According to Short, E.R. Bates of Bates Hardware Company supplied Maddox with 10,000 pick handles, exhausting the supplied of two local jobbers and five factories.

The bottom line is that Maddox could have kept his business simply by following the law of the land and serving food to another human being. He instead **chose** to put sixty-six people out of a job. He **chose** victim status. And he **chose** to profit by selling souvenirs based on the threat of physical violence against other human beings.

Maddox still faced trial on the gun-pointing incident. The case went to trial on April 12, 1965 in criminal court. According to Short, many people testified as character witnesses on behalf of Maddox including two ministers, one of whom was his own pastor at the North Atlanta Baptist Church. There was conflicting testimony as to whether Maddox pointed the gun or simply waived it. Maddox claimed he was acting in self-defense of his life and property – not acting to deny service to anyone.

It took an all-white jury 35 minutes to announce that Maddox was not guilty. Maddox never saw the irony in the fact that he benefited from the "system" against which he had railed for years in his advertisements. It would not be the last time.

The pick handle incident made Maddox a celebrity. Maddox was urged to parlay that celebrity status into a run for governor of Georgia. On September 25, 1965, Maddox announced his candidacy for the Democratic nomination for governor.

There were six candidates in the primary. The front-runner was former governor Ellis Arnall, an FDR Democrat. He had served as governor from 1943 to 1947. After his term he had angered Georgians by giving speeches indicating that Georgians were backward, poverty-stricken and poorly educated. Another candidate was Jimmy Carter. Maddox and three other candidates comprised the segregationist wing of the party. And Maddox was the biggest segregationist of them all.

In the primary, Arnall received 231,480 votes out of 787,952 votes cast. Maddox finished second with 185,672. Maddox would be in another runoff – this time with Ellis Arnall. Carter finished third.

Years later, Carter was quoted as saying that God had abandoned him twice in his life. The first was after the death of his father. The second was losing the 1966 gubernatorial primary. This was because Lester Maddox had beaten him (Jacobs, 1999). I haven't agreed with Carter on many things in the last 29 years, but I certainly agree with that statement. In the runoff, Carter's supporters, being mostly rural, broke for Maddox. Maddox won a resounding victory.

Mayor Ivan Allen, Jr. of Atlanta partially blamed Republicans for the Maddox victory. Crossover voting was allowed in primaries and Republicans were thought to have voted for Maddox in the runoff in order to have a week opponent for their candidate, Howard "Bo" Calloway.

The general election was held on November 8, 1966. Calloway defeated Maddox by 3,000 votes. However, 53,000 write-in votes for Arnall kept Calloway from receiving a majority. Under the Georgia constitution, the heavily Democratic legislature would elect the governor. Maddox was elected by a vote of 182–66.

Again, the political "system", Lester's target for so many years, had saved him.

I distinctly remember my father's reaction upon hearing that Maddox would be the governor of Georgia. "I don't know if I wish I had stayed to fight against it or if I'm just glad to not be in Georgia any longer", he said.

A search of the internet reveals many apologists for Maddox. Many people say he did more for blacks in Georgia than any previous governor. I am not qualified to speak to his accomplishments or failures in that job. One incident, however, stands out in my mind.

Maddox refused to attend the funeral of Martin Luther King, Jr. Maddox also refused to close state offices on the day of the funeral. The flags at the state capitol were at half-mast. He considered personally raising them. The presence of news cameras made him stop. As 200,000 mourners moved peacefully through downtown, Maddox holed up in the Capitol with 160 riot-helmeted state troopers, waiting for a riot that never happened.

In the 1970's, Maddox opened a souvenir shop in Underground Atlanta. He sold pick handles.

Maddox hid behind the shield of "states rights". He claimed to not be a racist. He was only a segregationist. Many people come to his defense on these issues. Nothing could be clearer to me than this: If you profit by selling mementos of threats of physical violence against someone based solely on the color of their skin, you are a racist. If you deny service or access to someone based solely on his or her skin color, you are a racist.

Maddox made an impression on me. He gave me a vivid image of a racist. I knew that I did not want to emulate his behavior.

CHAPTER 10
PERSONAL
DANGER

In My Father's House

The ice cream cone story, Deji Adejojin, and Lester Maddox all made lasting impressions on me. Nothing, however, compared to the realization that we lived in constant danger because of my father's actions and positions. It seemed so strange to me that people would want to harm us over this issue. We sang "Jesus loves the little children, all the children of the world" at church. That was probably the first song I learned. To me, my father was simply saying that we should believe the words of that song. How could we be in danger because of something so simple?

My father would sometimes include a prayer "for those who would do us harm" in his blessing at mealtime. Many times, my mother would answer the telephone and immediately stiffen. "May I ask who is calling?" she would say. After the caller would refuse to identify himself, she would say, "Well, if you won't tell me who you are, I'm not going to talk to you", and she would hang up. After we reached adulthood, Mom shared with us that many times the caller would say, "He must be out running around with his n___ girlfriend." She also told us, again in our adulthood, that many times she recognized the voices in spite of attempts to disguise them.

Most frightening were the drive-bys. We were acutely aware of cars that would drive slowly past our house. If this happened after dark, we would be instructed to turn off all the lights, move away from the front picture window, and get to the floor. The fear was that a bullet or Molotov cocktail would crash through the window.

One incident stood out above all others, however. As happened often, my mother, my sister and I were driving home from church after dark. On Wednesday evenings, Dad would stay at church after work instead of coming home. Mom would take us to church for the Wednesday evening meal and prayer meeting. On one such Wednesday evening, Mom realized that we were being followed as we drove home. My mother was a petite, shy southern woman. She had only begun driving in the early 1950's. All of a sudden she sped up and turned off the headlights. It was very dark. Her hope was that by turning off all lights, she could lose the pursuer while going around a bend in the road. Atlanta was, and is, famous for its curving roads. She was driving like the proverbial "bat out of hell."

I can still remember the fear approximately fifty years later. The knot in the pit of my stomach. The dry mouth. I was sure that whatever the pursuer was driving would be able to overtake our 1951 Buick sedan driven by my mother.

We were about a mile from home when Mom realized we were in danger. When we arrived at home, she turned into the driveway seemingly on two wheels. The garage was rear entry, so we came around to the back of the house and ran inside as if running for our lives. The car stopped at the curb in front and sat. We were afraid that Dad couldn't get home soon enough to save us while, at the same time, fearful of what this person might do to him when he arrived home. After what seemed like an eternity, the car drove away.

Mom never told Dad about the incident. He only learned of it at the time of her death in 2004. Prior to the visitation, the minister who would preside over the funeral gathered the family for a grief/remembrance session. I shared the "car chase" story as one of my chief memories of my mother. It was the first my father had heard of it.

Mom was painfully shy. She was never comfortable in the role of pastor's wife. But she had a way of rising to the occasion when her family was threatened. Dad has said that her encouragement and behavior were sources of great strength to him.

I have often wondered why the violence that befell others never was visited on our family. I know that the Klan was very aware of my father. Of course, anyone with access to the Atlanta newspapers would have been aware of Dad after 1956. But, in 1979, I found out in a humorous way that I had attended school with the daughter of Imperial Wizard James Venable.

I moved back to Atlanta in 1979. I was introduced to a lady with whom I had a couple of dates. During casual conversation on the first date, I mentioned that I had battled my weight all my life. I made a statement that I had made scores of times previously. "In school, I was always the second heaviest kid in my class", I said. Her response was "No you weren't. You were the heaviest." I was curious to know how she could make such a statement, and I was fully

convinced that she was wrong. She told me that we had
been in sixth grade together at Beecher Hills Elementary
School. Her name had not registered with me when we were
introduced since she was no longer using her maiden name.
She had been married and divorced and was still using her
married name. She, however, remembered me very well. I
had not been aware, in 1960-61, of her father's activities.
She had been aware of Dad, however. My father had been a
topic of conversation in their house. The next time I saw
Ginger, she produced a picture to prove that I had, indeed,
been the heaviest kid in the class.

Bob's sixth grade class picture from Beecher Hills Elementary School. Bob is
second from the left in the back row. Ginger Venable, daughter of James
Venable, Ku Klux Klan Imperial Wizard, is on the far left of the third row.

The Venable family had long owned Stone
Mountain. Sam Venable was the owner in 1914 when the
idea of the Confederate carving was hatched (ngeorgia.com,

2006). James Venable was an attorney and was a partner to Eldon Edwards in the Klan revival of the mid 1950's. He was also the owner of Stone Mountain (Quarles, 1999). Edwards died of a heart attack in 1960, and the Klan split into many factions. Robert Shelton subsequently controlled Klan activities in Alabama and James Venable held sway in Georgia (Chalmers, 1981). In 1962, three hundred Klansmen marched up Stone Mountain to protest the fact that the NAACP was holding its annual convention in Atlanta.

Unity meetings were held between Klan groups in Biloxi, MS and Atlanta. Chalmers gives credit to Venable for arranging these meetings:

> The main impetus for such meetings came not from Shelton and his United Klans and affiliates, but from the more chaotic followings of Atlanta attorney Jimmy Venable. Lacking Shelton's ability to organize things well, Venable opted for variety. In addition to his own National Knights, he had his Defensive League of Registered Americans, Inc., his Committee of One Million Caucasians to March on Washington, and his anti-Semitic boycotters, the Christian Voters and Buyers League. Most of the Klans that did not work with Shelton belonged to Venable's Federation of Klans (Chalmers, 1981, p. 376).

Venable's National Knights of the Ku Klux Klan of the 1960's and 1970's were not as violent as some Klans (Chalmers, 1981). He even defended blacks in court. He said he used the money they paid him to promote the Klan, but he claimed to defend them as vigorously as he defended the Klan (Southern Poverty Law Center, 2005). However, the Klan of the 1950's and early 1960's was violent, as outlined in Chapter 2.

Additionally, the owner of the barbershop in Cascade Heights was well known as a Klan official. My father and I were in that shop regularly for ten years. I don't remember seeing any barber other than the owner cut Dad's hair. Dad has said the he was unaware of this gentleman's Klan activities, but they were well known to both my sister and me. His daughter was a classmate of mine at Southwest High School and one of the best friends of my girlfriend.

I do not know why my family escaped violence. But I do know that it was threatened. I have asked my father how he felt about the risks for himself and his family. He says that he knew in 1936, when he felt called to the ministry, that a minister's life would involve risk. He did not know how those risks would manifest themselves. He knew that he could be asked to put his life on the line for the gospel. He did not know that he would take positions that would put his family at risk. But once he decided that the gospel required him to take a stand on racial issues, there seemed no alternative to him. Fairly or unfairly, he knew that he was also putting his family at risk – people who had no voice in the decisions. He did give my mother the opportunity to "opt out" three months before their wedding on the occasion of his birthday. He was beginning to assess the issue of risk in the ministry. Mom remained committed and always – although not always without complaint – supported Dad in his stances.

My father does not speak of specific threats. He does, when prompted, mention the exhortations of Lester

Maddox to "take care of" the people opposing forced segregation. He took those comments seriously.

As an adult, I have usually spoken up in protest when people make prejudicial remarks about any group of people. I have carried a slip of paper that reads: "Prejudice is the greatest labor-saving device known to man. You can form an opinion without having to do the research" (Anonymous). This has resulted in some spirited discussions. At some point in those discussions, I invariably point out that I was raised under threats of violence over the issue of prejudice. My sister, Karen, is a psychologist. She can cite studies that indicate that members of the majority ethnic group, when subjected to violence or threats of violence by other members of the majority, do not fully assimilate and accept the attitudes of the majority. I am thankful that this holds true in my case.

CHAPTER 11
RACE RELATIONS

In My Father's House

R obert C. Weaver delivered the following words in a
speech on June 13, 1963. Weaver would later
become the first African-American cabinet member
as the first Secretary of Housing and Urban Development in
President Johnson's administration:

> When the average well-informed white
> American discusses the issue of race with his
> negro counterpart, there are many areas of
> agreement. There are also certain areas of
> disagreement.
> Negro Americans usually feel that
> whites exaggerate progress; while whites
> frequently feel that negroes minimize gains.
> Then there are differences relative to the
> responsibility of negro leadership. It is in
> these areas of dispute that some of the most
> subtle and revealing aspects of black-white

153

relationships reside. And it is to the subtle and less obvious aspects of this problem that I wish to direct my remarks.

Most middle-class white Americans frequently ask, "Why do negroes push so? They have made phenomenal progress in 100 years of freedom, so why don't their leaders do something about the crime rate and illegitimacy?" (Essential Documents 1492–Present)

The entire text of Secretary Weaver's speech is attached as Exhibit E. It underscores that the issues of race relations are much the same today as they were in 1963.

These questions cut to the core of differences of perceptions between blacks and whites in today's society. I am ashamed to admit that I myself have used this argument many times. "Blacks have made so much progress. Look at the freedoms they enjoy now versus fifty years ago when I was growing up in the Deep South. Black leaders perpetuate their existence by playing up the victim status of blacks." Undoubtedly, much progress has been made – primarily in the area of open and full access to public facilities. But, in many respects, race relations – the relationships between people of different races – remain trapped in a 1950's time warp.

There are no race **relations** primarily because whites do not put themselves in positions to interact with people of color. And many whites, using standardized test scores and economic data, continue to argue that blacks are inferior. Yes, these differences exist, but whites need to wake up and realize that they are the result of discrepancies in opportunity – not an inherent, genetic discrepancy in ability.

A few years ago, my suburban, Protestant mega-church decided to start a new church in a joint venture with the largest African-American Methodist congregation in the Kansas City area. My church is located in the wealthiest county in the metropolitan area, and is virtually all white. The goal of the new congregation was to be multicultural and to be located in a fast growing suburb that, demographically, was more multicultural than my community. A request was made that thirty families make a commitment to worship at the new church, named Community of Hope, for one year. Five families from my church, out of over 3,000 member families, began worshipping at the new church. Two dropped out after the first month. I was one of the families who made and kept the commitment; and I was, at the time, a single man. Needless to say, the whites in my church did not put themselves in a position to interact with minorities.

After attending the new church for 1-½ years, I returned to my home church. It was 16 miles closer to my home, and I had sorely missed singing in the choir. I made friendships at Community of Hope, but my friendship with one particular couple, Pete and Roz Burney, has endured – even through their two-year residence in Massachusetts.

On one occasion, Pete and I were having dinner one evening when Roz was out of town. Pete asked me a question. "You were born and raised in Georgia, right? And you live in Johnson County, Kansas, right?" Pete already knew that the answer to both of these questions was "yes". "So it seems to me", Pete continued, "that you could have lived your whole life without having anything to do with black folk." Pete was really asking me why I didn't avoid blacks. Unspoken was "like most whites do."

I explained that I was raised to treat each person as an individual instead of focusing on differences. I had the opportunity to tell Pete of my father and some of my life experiences.

One experience, in particular, taught me that sometimes we have more in common with blacks than with other whites. One of those times was my first semester in college, at the University of Kansas.

My first day on campus at KU was a Sunday in the fall of 1967. My parents made sure I was settled – bed made and roommate met – before leaving. We arrived in mid-afternoon, my father having preached that morning. After they left, I had a rush of emotions. Pride, freedom, wonderment, awe and fear all mixed together. I knew no one other than the roommate I had just met. He was a smoker. I was not.

As evening approached, I found myself in the lobby of the dormitory – just milling around. I was drawn to a familiar face amidst the sea of unfamiliarity. It was the face of a drummer from my high school band. He was one of the five or six blacks in my graduating class out of a class of over 600. I had been the drum major of the band. There is a bond between the drum major and drummers in a marching band. His name was Richard. He was hanging out with one of the other blacks in my graduating class, Harold Lasley.

Richard was not housed in my dormitory, but Harold was. Harold would be in a room in the same wing of the dorm, but a couple of floors above me. I had not known Harold in high school. He was a jock, and I was a nerd. But there was an immediate bond in the fact that we came from the same high school.

We were to find one of the large auditoriums on campus the next morning to take a placement test. Harold and I decided to walk together. We were beginning a friendship.

Harold was rooming with a junior from Brooklyn, NY. I had never been around someone from New York. Even had I been raised a southern racist, I believe I would have chosen Harold's friendship over that of a New Yorker. This man was loud, talked incredibly fast and seemed pushier than anyone I had ever met. His most redeeming quality was that he owned a Four Tops album that he and Harold played frequently. I fell in love with the Four Tops. I eventually bought that album from Marvin. I still own it to this day.

Harold and I became fast friends quickly. We played basketball on the pickup lot behind the dorm. We went to the football games together. We ate meals together. Harold even attended church with me one Sunday and came to my house for a youth group luncheon. I never enjoyed a new friendship as much as I enjoyed my friendship with Harold.

But there was a problem. When Harold and I are our meals together in the dorm, no other blacks sat with us. The dorm was all male. KU did not allow co-ed dorms until the following year. There were approximately twelve blacks in our dorm. The blacks usually ate their meals together. I do not remember ever being invited to eat at the "black table." Harold was usually eating at a "white table."

Would I have been comfortable being the only white at a table? Probably not. It would have been a new situation for me. Harold, on the other hand, had been used to being one of the only blacks in a white world since his first day of school in Kansas City, KS in the fall of 1954.

This is another way in which times have not really changed. Whites are very used to the fact that blacks function with ease in a white world. Again, most whites come into contact with very few blacks.

Some blacks in the dorm began calling Harold an Uncle Tom because of his friendship with me. At first, it seemed that Harold deflected those comments with ease. But these were the 60's. Many blacks were becoming increasingly militant. Less than one year later, two black sprinters raised their fists in the Black Power salute while on the medal stand at the 1968 Mexico City Olympics. Increasingly, Harold distanced himself. By the start of the second semester, we had little contact. But I was given a gift in that experience. I learned that racial differences don't mean much when you long to see a familiar face. And racial differences pale in comparison to cultural differences.

I shared that story with Pete Burney at our dinner. I went so far as to tell him that, as two men raised in the South and transplanted to the Midwest, our differences were less than the inherent differences between men and women – even husbands and wives of the same race. I'm not sure Pete agreed with me. I could see him thinking about the experiences he has shared with Roz. Both experiencing living in the minority. Both hailing from the same, small town in Louisiana. I stand by my statement, however.

As I think about the inherent differences between men and women, I think of the callers to the sports talk shows I listen to on the radio. A large percentage of them are African-American men. Very few of them are women of any ethnicity. Men, of any race, are interested in cars, money, sports and sex – and not necessarily in that order. I then think of my beautiful wife and her interest in shoes, clothes, and hair and skin products. I think of the number of times she has used the good-natured defense of "I'm a woman" to explain inconsistencies in her behavior. Yes, I very much stand by my statement.

The lack of exposure that whites have to African-Americans was reinforced for me by an experience at the time of my marriage to Adriane. The best man at my wedding was a young man, by my standards, named Jeff Ostrander. I had known Jeff for about 10 years. At seventeen years my junior, Jeff was almost young enough to be my son. We are both very light haired and fair skinned. We have been asked on occasion if we are father and son. My standard response has been "No, but I wish he were my son." I have often referred to Jeff as the son I never had. When my son Bobby was born, he was given the middle name of Jeffrey. This was to honor the fact that Jeff and I are kindred spirits in many ways, especially spiritually and politically.

The ceremony was to be very small. Adriane was to have a maid of honor. Jeff would be my best man. Adriane's four children would be present. Jeff, the minister, Melanie (a friend of Adriane) and I were to be the only Caucasians at the wedding. Jeff called me the week prior to the wedding to express his nervousness about the ceremony. I couldn't imagine what could cause him to be anxious. He then told me that he had never had much experience around African-Americans. He had been raised in Tulsa, had attended Oklahoma State University in Stillwater, OK and worked in Dallas, TX before coming to Kansas City in 1992. My only reaction was "Wow". The ceremony came off without a hitch, and Jeff began to see that most of the differences are in our minds.

I do not attempt to assert that there are no differences between blacks and whites. I do assert, however, that those differences are cultural – just as the differences between

Harold's New York roommate and me. I need look no further for proof of my assertion than in the every day life of my own family.

My stepdaughter, Chantel Fulson, is a bright, stubborn, shy and messy fourteen-year-old girl. That makes her a pretty normal teenager – be she black, white, purple or pink. When Adriane and I were married, Chantel was in the last month of her 4th grade year in school. She had been in advanced education classes in her schools in Kansas City, KS, an inner-city school district. Louis Diuguid, a columnist at *The Kansas City Star* newspaper, has written an excellent book, A Teacher's Cry, about the challenges of that district. Adriane and I bought a house in Olathe, KS. Olathe is in Johnson County, KS, which is the most affluent county in the metropolitan area. We chose Olathe because it is **not** the most affluent area of the county, and we thought the schools in the area would be fairly diverse. There is a large Hispanic community in Olathe and the African-American population is well represented.

Chantel began her 5th grade school year in Olathe. She was not, however, placed into academically advanced classes. An assumption was made in Chantel's case that she would be challenged, academically, in Olathe schools because of the district from which she was transferring. Initially, her shyness seemed to validate this assessment. Thankfully, Chantel was blessed by her assignment to the classroom of a very patient, mature teacher. She saw past the shyness and worked to draw Chantel out of her shell. Chantel's academic gifts began to become apparent.

Chantel has just finished her first year of middle school – her 7th grade year. She has a 4.00-point GPA (grade point average) on a 4.00 scale. Her grades will not count toward college entry requirements until the 9th grade;

however, I see no reason to think that she can't continue her academic excellence at the same level (possible B's in physical education notwithstanding).

Similar experiences, though different in nature, have occurred with Alicia and Brandon. Alicia is a normal sixteen-year-old girl for whom school is a social event; clothes, music and fantasy video games are chief motivations. Alicia is the "blonde" of the family. Brandon is a twelve-year-old boy who is pushing his limits and is motivated by television and video games.

I long for people who believe in the inferiority of African-Americans to meet my family – especially Adriane. She is branch manager of a bank in Olathe. She is on the Board of Directors of the Olathe Public School Foundation and the Olathe Chamber of Commerce. She was a National Honor Society student in high school – something I was not. She is talented, bright, and articulate. She is a loving wife, mother and daughter. I believe she is capable of achieving any goal on which she sets her mind.

I think of the wide range of differences in the friendships and relationships I've had in my life. I think how much poorer my life would be had I limited my exposure to a certain type of person – be that personality type or ethnicity.

Many people reading this book will point to a certain experience in which they have been wronged or damaged by an African-American and scream that I am an apologist. Of them, I would ask "Haven't you ever been wronged by someone of your own race?" Many people will point to the challenges facing the African – American community, such as those mentioned in the speech earlier in this chapter. Again, I would ask, "Doesn't your race face challenges? Don't you personally face challenges?" It would take another book, longer than this one, to cover the wrongs inflicted on me by good, Caucasian, Christian, church goers. And I, personally, have faced challenges and fallen flat on many occasions. The true challenge is to get out of a comfort zone. Realize that each person is complete with gifts and faults. Their friendship could be a true treasure.

CHAPTER 12
LESSONS

W hat were the lessons I learned in my father's house? There are so many. Some of them I didn't know I learned – or maybe didn't remember – until adulthood. And that was after many starts, stops and failures. I learned lots of catch phrases: "If a job is worth doing, it's worth doing well." "Do unto others as you would have them do unto you." "To whom much is given, much is expected." I also memorized a lot of scripture verses: John 3:16; II Timothy 2:15; Romans 3:23; Matthew 28:19&20. I learned discipline. I learned the Ten Commandments. I learned that I was expected to make good grades.

But as I look back at my life, I realize that I learned one overriding lesson in my father's house. Each and every person on the face of this earth has value. Each person has a story of successes and failures. Each person has feelings. Each person has the same basic wants, desires and needs. And most importantly, each person is a child of God. Each person is loved by God and, if they are good enough for God, they sure as heck ought to be good enough for me.

I don't mean to infer that there aren't people who will harm me. Some people can't be trusted. There are some people of whom I should be wary. But we all started out the same way. Regardless of race or gender or nationality, we all started out naked as a jaybird and needing someone to keep us warm, dry, nourished and to love us. Some of us, like myself, had those needs met far more than others. And I will be eternally grateful to God and my parents for that.

I was fortunate to experience diversity in my father's house. Deiji Adejojin was Nigerian. A British evangelist held a revival meeting in our church and stayed in our house for the week or two of the revival. He burned a hole in our carpet using the hotplate Mom had provided him for the preparation of his tea at 6:00 a.m. (We did not rise that early in our house.) For years thereafter, my father and I drank hot tea with our breakfast. There was the lay preacher from Hungary who spoke at our church and ate a Sunday dinner at our house afterward. He told stories of how he escaped from under the heavy hand of Russian rule. A Chinese family in California hosted my father in a revival he preached in Los Angeles, using an interpreter during the sermons. I heard of this family for years. We even had Yankee preachers in our house from as far north as Louisville, KY. Now THAT was diversity for me.

Most people who have attained adulthood have been hurt in some way by someone. Vast numbers have generalized that all _____ (you fill in the blank) are "no good". I cannot help but think of my wife, my family, and the friends I would not have made had I been inclined to rule out African-Americans as inferior beings. The fact is that, in many ways, I cannot hold a candle to the intellectual and spiritual capabilities of the blacks that have touched my life. But many people who have generalized their hurts will read this book and think I am crazy.

I cannot help but wonder what people who hold views of prejudice and superiority think they did to cause and/or earn birth into a certain race/gender/nationality/creed. I was not born to money. As a child I bemoaned that fact. But, with apologies to the "angry white man", I was born a white male in the United States of America – the country in the world with the most freedoms. I have told friends since 1990 to slap me if they ever hear me "crying the blues." America in 1949 was a country dominated by white males. I won the lottery. I can think of nothing I did to earn such status, nor can I think of anything I did to deserve such a blessing.

In spite of all I learned while growing up, the nature of that blessing was reinforced in a very personal way when I married Adriane. My father developed an interest in genealogy in the 1980's. I must confess that I did not share that interest. Both of my grandfathers died years before I was born. We had not come from royalty or money. I didn't see the point. I did, however, become interested in Dad's research after I realized that there is a hole in Adriane's soul. That is what I call it. That hole exists because she knew very little about her family beyond her parents' generation. She remembered her grandparents, but knew very little about their histories.

As I delved into Dad's research, I learned that I could trace my lineage to 1660. Thomas Shands, born in that year, came to Virginia from Scotland in 1674 as Secretary to the Clerk of the House of Burgesses of Virginia, James Minge. The first Shands in my line to be born in America was

William, born in 1685. My lineage is unbroken from that time. My brother, sister and I are the tenth generation of Shands born in America. I then researched Adriane's lineage. We have been able to document information about her great-grandparents. We have a paper trail to approximately 1880. The harsh reality is that the trail probably stops there because of slavery. Her great-great grandparents would have been born during the slave years.

When William Shands died, his estate consisted of three slaves: Yellow Face, Dick, and Bob. They were bequeathed to his son, John. Because of slavery, my wife cannot trace her roots farther than three generations. I have heard many whites say that slavery was so long ago that it has no effect on the current generation. I would have to disagree.

As I mentioned, one of the catch phrases I learned was "To whom much is given, much is expected." I did not fully understand why my father kept saying that. Our needs were met, but we certainly had less money and toys than my friends. It seems that the context in which Dad used this phrase was, more often than not, when I was complaining about the lack of quality family time we had. I felt that I was *always* at church. And when we weren't at church Dad was usually gone in the evening attending a meeting. We were told that, as a minister's family, we were called to sacrifice.

I had many conversations with my father during the writing of this book. He always downplayed the significance of his actions by saying "I was just doing my job". But it is clear that other ministers did not consider social justice part of their job. He usually minimized the danger he felt. But one statement he made to me clarified, in my mind, the degree of sacrifice of time he, and by extension our family, made. He said that, after the Georgia Baptist Convention in 1956, events were happening at a whirlwind pace and each day was an exercise in "keeping up." I visualize a man caught in a whirlpool of water – frantically trying to keep his head above the surface. Perhaps a better analogy would be that of a juggler. He was juggling the reactions of the general public, other ministers, and his congregation.

The issues of social justice probably never left his mind. He was aware that much had been given to him in relation to a whole race of people who were fighting for the right to drink out of a clean water fountain and take any seat on a bus. Much had been given to him, and he was giving back his most precious possessions – his time and the Gospel.

Relative to my father, I was slow to realize that my skin color was a blessing. Many whites with whom I have argued simply consider it a birthright and symbol of superiority – both intellectually and morally. To them I have one piece of advice. Be a landlord. I once had the responsibility to lease and manage 300 apartment units and 100,000 square feet of office space in Atlanta. These properties ranged from government subsidized Section 8 housing to upscale town homes and boutiques in affluent areas of North Atlanta. Some were in blue-collar areas of town. And the lessons of diversity I learned from my father were reinforced in a much different manner.

The lowest and most base behavioral traits of mankind make no distinction across racial or gender lines. Lying, destruction of property, theft, and rent-skipping in the dark of night are human traits. They are not confined to a particular race, gender, national origin or creed. They occur across economic lines, as well. If I had harbored racist thoughts, my days as a landlord would surely have erased any thoughts that my race made me superior.

In the preface of this book, I wrote that the memory of the Jim Crow South must not die. I also wrote that it could happen again. In 2005, Hurricane Katrina heightened racial tensions. As I watched the first television image of looting in New Orleans I told Adriane, that this storm had the potential to set race relations in this country back fifty years. The attempt to organize a Klan in Olathe stated a goal of promoting "white Christianity." I didn't know there was such a thing.

Any cursory Internet search will reveal newsgroups with "n_____" in the title. Such message boards vilify blacks and spew venom. Essays promoting a return to slavery receive a substantial number of rave reviews. It is folly to think that prejudice in America will be eradicated. Some group is always the target of prejudice: Jews, Catholics, Irish, Italians, Hungarians, blacks. But I, for one, will not be guilty of the "sin of silence," as Dr. Roy McClain called it in his book so many years ago. I cannot turn my back on the legacy of my father. I cannot turn my back on my wife, my stepchildren or my son. And I cannot turn my back on Christ's admonition to "love your neighbor as yourself."

Another major lesson I learned in my father's house is that the Bible is open to interpretation. How else could ministers have taken such diverse positions on segregation as was evident in Atlanta in 1957? The religious right will tell you that every word in the Bible is true and is the written word of God. They will tell you that the Bible is **not** open to interpretation. Of them I ask "Whose interpretation was correct in Atlanta in the 1950's?" Which part of the Bible was the true word of God? I have tried to steer clear of preaching and theologizing in this book. I am not qualified.

I am, however, qualified to speak to the human frailties of ministers. It should be obvious that I love and respect my father. I believe that my father truly lived out a calling from God. But I also know that he is human. He would be the first to admit that. But, having grown up as a "PK" (preacher's kid), I cultivated a keen interest in, and observation of, ministers at an early age. And I can tell you that ministers struggle with the same temptations of the flesh and spirit that challenge us all. Perhaps the biggest temptation that ministers face is that of ego. They stand up in front of congregations each week and speak the Truth. They tell congregants what is right and what is wrong. And they begin to believe in their infallibility. Church growth, larger buildings, television contracts and book deals become a focus.

Lastly, I learned that God has a sense of humor. I think of all of the effort that the deacons of West End Baptist Church made to keep worship segregated. I think of that beautiful sanctuary that was not open to people of color. And I think of how people of color worship every Sunday in that sanctuary today.

West End Baptist Church disbanded in 1971. The physical facilities were sold to the Hunter Street Baptist Church, which is now known as the West Hunter Street Baptist Church. Ralph David Abernathy, first lieutenant to Martin Luther King, Jr., was the pastor of Hunter Street Baptist Church. The address I knew, 1040 Gordon Street, is now 1040 Ralph Abernathy Blvd.

Along the same lines, the home of James Venable was purchased in 1996 by an African-American couple, Chuck Burris and Marcia Baird Burris. Chuck Burris became the first African-American mayor of Stone Mountain. *Ebony* magazine published a wonderful article in October of 1998 about the mayor and how he came to own Venable's house. Ginger handled the transaction. When the Burrises moved in, Ginger commented that the roses were in bloom for the first time in five years.

My father taught me well. I hope I learned nearly as well as he taught. And I trust I can pass his lessons along to my children and all of Mom & Dad's grandchildren and great-grandchildren. May we all constantly assess our attitudes toward all people and work toward a greater level of tolerance and understanding in our society.

EXHIBITS

EXHIBIT A

THE DECISION OF THE SUPREME COURT IN THE SCHOOL CASES – DECLARATION OF CONSTITUTIONAL PRINCIPLES.

Mr. (Walter F.) George.   Mr. President, the increasing gravity of the situation following the decision of the Supreme Court in the so-called segregation cases, and the peculiar stress in sections of the country where this decision has created many difficulties, unknown and unappreciated, perhaps, by many people residing in other parts of the country, have led some Senators and some Members of the House of Representatives to prepare a statement of the position which they have felt and now feel to be imperative.

I now wish to present to the Senate a statement on behalf of 19 Senators, representing 11 States, and 77 House Members, representing a considerable number of States likewise . . .

DECLARATION OF PRINCIPLES

The unwarranted decision of the Supreme Court in the public school cases is now bearing the fruit always produced when men substitute naked power for established law.

The Founding Fathers gave us a Constitution of checks and balances because they realized the inescapable lesson of history that no man or group of men can be safely entrusted with unlimited power. They framed this Constitution with its provisions for change by amendment in order to secure the fundamentals of government against the dangers of temporary popular passion or the personal predilections of public officeholders.

We regard the decisions of the Supreme Court in the school cases as a clear abuse of judicial power. It climaxes a trend in the Federal Judiciary undertaking to legislate, in derogation of the authority of Congress, and to encroach upon the reserved rights of the States and the people.

The original Constitution does not mention education. Neither does the 14th Amendment nor any other amendment. The debates preceding the submission of the 14th Amendment clearly show that there was no intent that it should affect the system of education maintained by the States.

The very Congress which proposed the amendment subsequently provided for segregated schools in the District of Columbia.

When the amendment was adopted in 1868, there were 37 States of the Union . . . .

Every one of the 26 States that had any substantial racial differences among it people, either approved the operation of segregated schools already in existence or subsequently established such schools by action of the same law-making body which considered the 14th Amendment.

As admitted by the Supreme Court in the public school case (*Brown* v. *Board of Education*), the doctrine of separate but equal schools "apparently originated in *Roberts* v. *City of*

Boston (1849), upholding school segregation against attack as being violative of a State constitutional guarantee of equality." This constitutional doctrine began in the North, not in the South, and it was followed not only in Massachusetts, but in Connecticut, New York, Illinois, Indiana, Michigan, Minnesota, New Jersey, Ohio, Pennsylvania and other northern states until they, exercising their rights as states through the constitutional processes of local self-government, changed their school systems.

In the case of *Plessy* v. *Ferguson* in 1896 the Supreme Court expressly declared that under the 14th Amendment no person was denied any of his rights if the States provided separate but equal facilities. This decision has been followed in many other cases. It is notable that the Supreme Court, speaking through Chief Justice Taft, a former President of the United States, unanimously declared in 1927 in *Lum* v. *Rice* that the "separate but equal" principle is "within the discretion of the State in regulating its public schools and does not conflict with the 14th Amendment."

This interpretation, restated time and again, became a part of the life of the people of many of the States and confirmed their habits, traditions, and way of life. It is founded on elemental humanity and commonsense, for parents should not be deprived by Government of the right to direct the lives and education of their own children.

Though there has been no constitutional amendment or act of Congress changing this established legal principle almost a century old, the Supreme Court of the United States, with no legal basis for such action, undertook to exercise their naked judicial power and substituted their personal political and social ideas for the established law of the land.

This unwarranted exercise of power by the Court, contrary to the Constitution, is creating chaos and confusion in the States principally affected. It is destroying the amicable relations between the white and Negro races that have been created through 90 years of patient effort by the good people of both races. It has planted hatred and suspicion where there has been heretofore friendship and understanding.

Without regard to the consent of the governed, outside mediators are threatening immediate and revolutionary changes in our public schools systems. If done, this is certain to destroy the system of public education in some of the States.

With the gravest concern for the explosive and dangerous condition created by this decision and inflamed by outside meddlers:

We reaffirm our reliance on the Constitution as the fundamental law of the land.

We decry the Supreme Court's encroachment on the rights reserved to the States and to the people, contrary to established law, and to the Constitution.

We commend the motives of those States, which have declared the intention to resist forced integration by any lawful means.

We appeal to the States and people who are not directly affected by these decisions to consider the constitutional principles involved against the time when they too, on issues vital to them may be the victims of judicial encroachment.

Even though we constitute a minority in the present Congress, we have full faith that a majority of the American people believe in the dual system of government which has enabled us to achieve our greatness and will in time demand that reserved rights of the States and of the people be made secure against judicial usurpation.

We pledge ourselves to use all lawful means to bring about a reversal of this decision, which is contrary to the Constitution, and to prevent the use of force in its implementation.

In this trying period, as we all seek to right this wrong, we appeal to our people not to be provoked by the agitators and troublemakers invading our States and to scrupulously refrain from disorder and lawless acts.

Signed by:

MEMBERS OF THE UNITED STATES SENATE

Walter F. George, Richard B. Russell, John Stennis, Sam J. Ervin, Jr., Strom Thurmond, Harry F. Byrd, A. Willis Robertson, John L. McClellan, Allen J. Ellender, Russell B. Long, Lister Hill, James O. Eastland, W. Kerr Scott, John Sparkman, Olin D. Johnston, Price Daniel, J.W. Fulbright, George A. Smathers, Spessard L. Holland.

Exhibit A

MEMBERS OF THE UNITES STATES HOUSE OF REPRESENTATIVES

Alabama: Frank W. Boykin, George M. Grant, George W. Andrews, Kenneth A. Roberts, Albert Rains, Armistead I. Selden, Jr., Carl Elliott, Robert E. Jones, George Huddleston, Jr.

Arkansas: E.C. Gathings, Wilbur D. Mills, James W. Trimble, Oren Harris, Brooks Hays, W.F. Norrell.

Florida: Charles E. Bennett, Robert L.F. Sikes, A.S. Herlong, Jr., Paul G. Rogers, James A. Haley, D.R. Matthews.

Georgia: Prince H. Preston, John L. Pilcher, E.L. Forrester, John James Flynt, Jr., James C. Davis, Carl Vinson, Henderson Lanham, Iris F. Blitch, Phil M. Landrum, Paul Brown.

Louisiana: F. Edward Herbert, Hale Boggs, Edwin E. Willis, Overton Brooks, Otto E. Passman, James H. Morrison, T. Ashton Thompson, George S. Long.

Mississippi: Thomas G. Abernathy, Jamie L. Whitten, Frank E. Smith, John Bell Williams, Arthur Winstead, William M. Colmer.

North Carolina: Herbert C. Bonner, L.H. Fountain, Graham A. Barden, Carl T. Durham, F. Ertel Carlyle, Hugh Q. Alexander, Woodrow W. Jones, George A. Shuford.

Exhibit A

South Carolina: L. Mendel Rivers, John J. Riley, W.J. Bryan Dorn, Robert T. Ashmore, James P. Richards, John L. McMillan.

Tennessee: James B. Frazier, Jr., Tom Murray, Jere Cooper, Clifford Davis.

EXHIBIT B

**List of pastoral essays on racial tensions in 1957
All published in *The Atlanta Journal and Constitution***

- Conversion, Not Force Answer to Racial Issue – October 13,1957. Dr. Roy O. McClain – Pastor, First Baptist Church of Atlanta

- Tolerance and Discussion Keys to Racial Problem, Minister Says – October 20, 1957. Rev. Harry A. Fifield – Minister, First Presbyterian Church

- City's Racial Approach Offers Signs of Hope, Minister Says – October 27, 1957. Dr. Dow Kirkpatrick – Minister, St. Mark Methodist Church

- Respect Called Christian Duty – November 3, 1957. Rev. Harry Tisdale – Rector, Holy Trinity Episcopal Church of Decatur, GA

- Disturbing Truth Element in Pulpit Paralysis Charge – November 10, 1957. Rev. Robert E. Lee – Pastor, Lutheran Church of the Redeemer

- Moses, Prophets, Jesus Fought to Erase Inequality – November 17, 1957. Rabbi Jacob M. Rothschild of The Temple, Atlanta

Exhibit B

- Bible Orders Separation and Love – November 24, 1957. Rev. J.W. Harwell – Pastor, Bethany Baptist Church, Madison, GA

- Segregation Called Social Rather Than Moral Issue – December 1, 1957. Rev. George O. King – Pastor, First Methodist Church of East Point, GA

- Household of Faith Offers Solution to Racial Problem – December 8, 1957. Dr. Thomas A. Fry, Jr. – Pastor, Druid Hills Presbyterian Church of Atlanta

- Minister Says He Cannot Defend Segregated Society – December 15, 1957. Rev. Harrison McMains – Executive Director, Christian Council of Atlanta

- Judgment of God is Upon Enforced Segregation – December 22, 1957. Dr. Norman Shands – Pastor, West End Baptist Church

- Poverty of Faith in God Finds U.S. in Sick World – December 29, 1957. Rev. A.E. Fortune – Pastor, Rice Memorial Presbyterian Church, U.S. (Colored)

- Doctrine of Segregation Plainly Taught in Bible – January 5, 1958. Rev. Billy S. Cobb – Pastor, Dunwoody Baptist Church

EXHIBIT C

The Atlanta Journal and Constitution
– December 22, 1957

A BAPTIST LEADER SPEAKS

"Judgment of God is Upon Enforced Segregation"
Dr. Norman Shands – Pastor, West End Baptist Church

That moral and spiritual principles are involved in the present crisis in race relations, no thoughtful person will deny. This fact gives every minister a Divine directive to speak out boldly, even though there are sharp differences of opinion. Phillip Brooks once said, "No powerful pulpit ever held aloof from the moral life of the community it lives in... When a strong, clear issue stands out plain, the preacher has his duty as sharply marked as that of the soldier on the field of battle."

A minister has the responsibility to guide the members of his congregation to a full understanding of God's will concerning their social, economic, and political relationships. The Old and New Testament make it abundantly clear that no man can be in right relationship to God and in wrong relationship to his fellow man at the same time. Throughout the Bible, love to God and love to one's neighbor are described as man's highest duty. Because the way a man treats his neighbor is vitally involved in the current crisis, moral and spiritual judgments must be made.

Exhibit C

Ultimately these judgments must be made by the people as a whole, not dictated by their leaders. At the same time their leaders are responsible before God for the influence of their thought and example. With this in view the writer presumes to share with a wider audience the convictions concerning God's will in our current crisis that have been proclaimed consistently to his own congregation.

The Gospel of the Kingdom of God lays two simple requirements on all man viz repentance and faith. This means that God will not allow us to identify our little systems and schemes with the Kingdom of God. Neither the "American Way of Life," the "Southern Way of Life," the "Northern Way of Life," the "Georgia Way of Life,' the way of capitalism, of communism, nor any middle way are synonymous with the Kingdom of God. The heart of idolatry is the effort of man to make himself a god in his own image. True religion requires humility and faith before their infinite God who has made man in His image.

Thus every system of man falls under the judgment of God. His judgment is upon enforced segregation. Even its most ardent supporters, according to all reports, admit privately that its days are numbered. They only hope to postpone its demise. Likewise the judgment of God is upon enforced integration. Its most ardent supporters are more uncertain than they were 12 months ago. Both of these systems fall short of God's will because there is something in each which is contrary to the nature of man as God created him.

The highest law men are required to follow is not the Constitution of the United States, but the royal law of love. A Hebrew prophet in the eighth century B.C. wrote:

Exhibit C

"He has showed you, O man, what is good; and what does the Lord require of you but to do justice, and to love kindness, and to walk humbly with your God?" Micah 6:8 (RSV).

A Hebrew Christian of the first century A.D. wrote:

If you really fulfill the royal law according to scripture, "You shall love your neighbor as yourself", you do well, but if you show partiality, you commit sin, and are convicted by the law as transgressors. For whoever keeps the whole law but fails in one point has become guilty of all of it, for he who said, "Do not commit adultery, also said, Do not kill. If you do not commit adultery but do kill you have become a transgressor of the law. So speak and so act as those who are to be judged under the law of liberty. For judgment is without mercy to one who has shown no mercy; yet mercy triumphs over judgment. James 2:8–13 (RSV).

This does not mean, however, that the Christian citizen can, in good conscience, be indifferent to the law or rebellious against the courts that administer it. It means that he will honor the authority of his government and respect its laws at all points except where they may violate his conscience or compel him to act contrary to God's will. At such points he will work peacefully and lawfully for the change of such laws or yield himself peacefully to the penalty of disobedience, registering his protest. This is in keeping with Christ's instruction to render to Caesar that

Exhibit C

which is Caesar's and to God that which is God's. It is also harmonious with Paul's discussion of civil authority in Romans 13. Any other course encourages anarchy, which would destroy all order and with it all personal liberty. No sincere Christian will knowingly advocate or encourage violence and anarchy as the solution to any problem, however delicate it may be.

The Christian citizen recognizes that the authority of the law rests, not upon the wisdom of men or upon the institutions of man, but upon the moral law of God. This law is written into the nature of the universe and of man. This is forthrightly declared in the most famous sentence of the Declaration of Independence. Following an appeal to the "Laws of Nature and of Nature's God", it says:

> We hold these truths to be self-evident, that all men are created equal, that they are endowed by their Creator with certain inalienable rights, that among these are Life, Liberty and the Pursuit of Happiness.

Thus, the concept of law on which our nation was founded recognizes that its basic authority is founded on the revealed moral and spiritual laws of God. If we are to survive as a nation, we must depart from the concept of moral relativism and return to a recognition of Divine authority. Ultimately, acts of Congress, Executive orders, Supreme Court decisions, and acts of State and local officials will stand or fall in accordance with their harmony with Divine laws. Christian citizens will be found praying that in the process of the inevitable tensions and conflicts between these legal entities of government, the end result

Exhibit C

will be in accord with God's will. This will be just for all men regardless of race or class.

While such tensions are being worked out, Christian citizens of all viewpoints might profitably consider the following attitudes and actions:

1. Humble recognition of one's own imperfections and sins and those of the society in which he lives.
2. Set example of love and respect for all men as those who are made in the image of God.
3. Encourage respect for law and for the authority of the courts in matters pertaining to law, while asserting at the same time the supremacy of the laws of God and the liberty of the individual conscience under God.
4. Accept the decision of the Supreme Court, in so far as it strikes down legislation that compels segregation, as consistent with the laws of God.
5. Work for interpretations and implementations of this decision, which would eliminate all attempts to enforce integration, leaving the maximum opportunity for voluntary choice on the part of students and parents.
6. Enlarge personal knowledge of the Bible and improve personal witness to the truth of God, as it is now understood.

Exhibit C

The greatest danger today is that fear will drive us to hysterical and stupid extremes. This danger seems to be less now than it was 12 months ago. The mass of people has been awakened to the peril by the extreme attitudes of some. The logical and reasonable approach of our senators during the discussions of the civil rights bill helped to restore reason and to gain wider understanding of the problems. Ministers and laymen are discovering a growing appreciation of their witness to moral and spiritual principles. There is a growing humility and prayerfulness in many segments of the population. More and more Christian citizens will, I am sure, work in the confidence that faith in God and in one another will enable us to follow the royal law of love. This alone can lead us out of a wilderness of fear and hate.

EXHIBIT D

"MINISTERS' MANIFESTO"

80 ATLANTA PASTORS SIGN MANIFESTO ON RACIAL BELIEFS

The Atlanta Journal and Constitution
Sunday, November 3, 1957

Here is a complete text of a statement issued by a group of Atlanta ministers on race relations.

These are days of tremendous political and social tension throughout our entire world, but particularly in our nation and beloved Southland. The issues which we face are not simple nor can they be resolved overnight. Because the questions which confront us are in so many respects moral and spiritual as well as political, it is appropriate and necessary that men who occupy places of responsibility in the churches should not be silent concerning their convictions.

The signers of this statement are all ministers of the Gospel, but we speak also as citizens of Georgia and of the United States of America. We are all Southerners, either by birth or by choice, and speak as men who love the South, who seek to understand its problems, and who are vitally concerned for its welfare.

In preparing this statement we have acted as individuals, and represent no one but ourselves. At the same time we believe that the sentiments which we express are shared by a multitude of our fellow citizens, who are deeply troubled by our present situation and who know that hatred, defiance and violence are not the answer to our problems, but who have been without a voice and have found no way to make their influence effective.

IN PRESENTING our views for the consideration of others we can speak only in a spirit of deep humility and of penitence for our own failures. We cannot claim that the problem of racial relationships has been solved even in the churches which we serve and we are conscious that our own example in the matter of brotherhood and neighborliness has been all too imperfect. We do not pretend to know all the answers.

We are of one mind, however, in believing that Christian people have an especial responsibility for the solution of our racial problems and that if, as Christians, we sincerely seek to understand and apply the teachings of our Lord and Master we shall assuredly find the answer.

We do not believe that the South is more to blame than are other areas of our nation for the difficulties which we face. The presence of the Negro in America is the result of the infamous slave traffic – an evil for which the North was as much responsible as the South.

WE ARE ALSO conscious that racial injustice and violence are not confined to our section and that racial problems have by no means been solved anywhere in our nation. Two wrongs, however, do not make a right. The failures of others are not a justification for our own shortcomings, nor can their unjust criticisms excuse us for a failure to do our duty in the sight of God. Our one concern must be to know and to do that which is right.

We believe that the difficulties before us have been greatly increased by extreme attitudes and statements on both sides. The use of the word "integration" in connection with our schools and other areas of life has been unfortunate, since to many that term has become synonymous with amalgamation. We do not believe in the amalgamation of the races, nor do we feel that it is favored by right thinking members of either race.

We do believe that all Americans, whether black or white, have a right to the full privileges of first class citizenship. To suggest that a recognition of the rights of Negroes to the full privileges of American citizenship, and to such necessary contacts as might follow would inevitably result in intermarriage is to cast as serious and unjustified an aspersion upon the white race as upon the Negro race.

Believing as we do in the desirability of preserving the integrity of both races through the free choice of both, we would emphasize the following principles which we hold to be of basic importance for our thought and conduct:

1. FREEDOM of speech must at all costs be preserved "Truth is mighty and will prevail." No minister, editor, teacher, state employee, business man or other citizen should be penalized for expressing himself freely, so long as he does so with due regard to the rights of others. Any position which cannot stand upon its own merits and which can only be maintained by silencing all who hold contrary convictions, is a position which cannot permanently endure.

2. AS AMERICANS and as Christians we have an obligation to obey the law. This does not mean that all loyal citizens need approve the 1954 decision of the Supreme Court with reference to segregation in the public schools. Those who feel that this decision was in error have every right to work for an alteration in the decree, either through a

further change in the Supreme Court's interpretation of the law, or through an amendment to the Constitution of the United States. It does mean that we have no right to defy the constituted authority in the government of our nation. Assuredly also it means that resorts to violence and to economic reprisals as a means to avoid the granting of legal rights to other citizens are never justified.

3. THE PUBLIC school system must not be destroyed. It is an institution essential to the preservation and development of our democracy. To sacrifice that system in order to avoid obedience to the decree of the Supreme Court would be to inflict tremendous loss upon multitudes of children, whose whole lives would be impoverished as a result of such action. It would also mean the economic, intellectual and cultural impoverishment of our section, and would be a blow to the welfare of our nation as a whole.

4. HATRED and scorn for those of another race, or for those who hold a position different from our own, can never be justified. It is only as we approach our problems in a spirit of mutual respect of charity, and of good will that we can hope to understand one another, and to find the way to a cooperative solution of our problems. God is no respecter of persons. Every human personality is precious in His sight. No policy which seeks to keep any man from developing fully every capacity of body, mind and of spirit can be justified in the light of scripture. This is the message of the Hebrew prophets as it is of Christ and His disciples. We shall solve our difficulties when we learn to walk in obedience to the Golden Rule: "Therefore, all things, whatsoever you would that men should do to you, do ye even so to them for this is the law and the prophets."

5. COMMUNICATION between responsible leaders of the races must be maintained. One of the tragedies of our

present situation is found in the fact that there is so little real discussion of the issues except within the separate racial groups. Under such circumstances it is inevitable that misunderstandings will continue and that suspicion and distrust will be encouraged. One of the reasons that extreme measures have been so often proposed or adopted by groups within both races is found in the fact that those who are most concerned have seldom faced the issues in a situation where there could be a free exchange of ideas. We believe that a willingness of the part of white leaders to talk with leaders of the Negro race, and to understand what those leaders are really seeking for their people is necessary and desirable. An expressed willingness on our part to recognize their needs, and to see that they are granted their full rights as American citizens, might lead to a cooperative approach to the problem which would provide equal rights and yet maintain the integrity of both races upon a basis of mutual esteem and of free choice rather than of force.

6. OUR DIFFICULTIES cannot be solved in our own strength or in human wisdom. It is appropriate, therefore, that we approach our task in a spirit of humility, of penitence, and of prayer. It is necessary that we pray earnestly and consistently that God will give us wisdom to understand His will; that He will grant us the courage and faith to follow the guidance of His Spirit.

To such prayer and obedience we would dedicate ourselves and summon all men of good will.

Exhibit D

SIGNERS OF STATEMENT

This is an alphabetical list of Atlanta ministers signing the declaration of beliefs on the racial problems:

Wallace M. Alston
Charles L. Allen
Thomas Anderson
Raymond J. Ball
Wade H. Boggs
Jack Bozeman
Lee Branham
W.C. Budd
A.L. Burgreen
Robert W. Burns
C.W. Carpenter
Randolph R. Claiborne Jr.
Lamar Clements
Samuel T. Cobb
E. Dudley Colhoun
Vance Daniel
Eugene Drinkard
Edward Driscoll
L.B. Ellington
D.J. Evans
Harry Fifeld
Emmett Floyd
Austin Ford
J.T. Ford
Thomas A. Fry Jr.
John Garber
Arthur Vann Gibson

Victor A. Greene
Victor L.Griggs
Thomas Hagood
Alfred Hardman
DickH. Hall Jr.
Claud M. Haynes
W. I. Howell
Herbert Hyde
Bevel Jones
Dow Kirkpatrick
Robert E. Kribbs
Edward Lantz
Robert E. Lee
Fitzhugh M. Legerton
John Blix Lind
Nat G. Long
James D. Matthews
Roy O. McClain
Harrison McMains
W. Robert Mill
Harold W. Minor Jr.
Harry L. Mitcham
Walter Murphy
William E. Newton
Stuart Oglesby
Robert Ozment
Roy Pettway
J. Davison Philips

Paul Renz
J. McDowell Richards
Frank M. Ross
E.D. Rudisill
Lester Rumble
Hugh Saussy Jr
Charles F. Schwab
O. Norman Shands
Rembert Sisson
W. Thomas Smith
Wilson Sneed
R. H. Stewart
Monroe F. Swilley Jr.
James W. Sosebee
W. Earl Strickland
Harry Tisdale
Herman L. Turner
L.F. VanLandingham
Wendell Wellman
Albert Wells
Charles L. Widney
Allison Williams
Eugene T. Wilson
John Womack
Milton L. Wood

EXHIBIT E

THE NEGRO AS AN AMERICAN

June 13, 1963

Speech by Robert C. Weaver who would become the first African-American cabinet member: Secretary of Housing and Urban Development in the Johnson administration.

When the average well-informed and well-intentioned white American discusses the issue of race with his negro counterpart, there are many areas of agreement. There are also certain significant areas of disagreement.

Negro Americans usually feel that whites exaggerate progress; while whites frequently feel that negroes minimize gains. Then there are differences relative to the responsibility of negro leadership. It is in these areas of dispute that some of the most subtle and revealing aspects of negro-white relationships reside. And it is to the subtle and less obvious aspects of this problem that I wish to direct my remarks.

Most middle-class white Americans frequently ask, "Why do negroes push so? They have made phenomenal progress in 100 years of freedom, so why don't their leaders do something about the crime rate and illegitimacy?" To them I would reply that when negroes press for full equality now, they are behaving as all other Americans would under similar circumstances. Every American has the right to be treated as a human being, and striving for human dignity is a national characteristic. Also, there is nothing inconsistent in such action and realistic self-appraisal. Indeed, as I shall develop, self-help programs among non-whites, if they are to be effective, must go hand-in-glove with the opening of new opportunities.

Negroes who are constantly confronted or threatened by discrimination and inequality articulate a sense of outrage. Many react with hostility, sometimes translating their feelings into overt anti-social actions. In parts of the negro community, a separate culture with deviant values develops. To the members of this subculture, I would observe that ours is a middle-class society, and those who fail to evidence most of its values and behavior are headed toward difficulties. But I am reminded that the rewards for those who do are often minimal, providing insufficient inducement for large numbers to emulate them.

Until the second decade of the twentieth century, it was traditional to compare the then current position of negroes with that of a decade or several decades ago. The depression revealed the basic marginal economic status of colored Americans and repudiated this concept of progress. By the early 1930's, negroes became concerned about their relative position in the nation.

Of course, there are those who observe that the average income, the incidence of home ownership, the rate of acquisition of automobiles, and the like, among negroes in the United States are higher than in some so-called advanced nations. Such comparisons mean little. Incomes are significant only in relation to the cost of living, and the other attainments and acquisitions are significant for comparative purposes only when used to reflect the negro's relative position in the world. The negro here – as he has so frequently and eloquently demonstrated – is an American. And his status, no less than his aspirations, can be measured meaningfully only in terms of American standards.

Viewed from this point of view, what are the facts?

Median family income among non-whites was slightly less than 55 percent of that for whites in 1959; for individuals, the figure was 50 percent.

Only a third of the negro families in 1959 earned sufficient (incomes) to sustain an acceptable American standard of living. Yet, this involved well over a million negro families, of which 6,000 earned $25,000 or more.

Undergirding these overall figures are many paradoxes. Negroes have made striking gains in historical terms, yet their current rate of unemployment is well over double that among whites. Over two-thirds of our colored workers are still concentrated in five major unskilled and semi-skilled occupations, as contrasted to slightly over a third of the white labor force.

Despite the continuing existence of color discrimination, even for many of the well prepared, there is a paucity of qualified negro scientists, engineers, mathematicians, and highly trained clerical and stenographic workers. Lack of college-trained persons is especially evident among negro men. One is prompted to ask why does this exist?

In 1959, non-white males who were high school graduates earned, on the average, 32 percent less than whites; for non-white college graduates, the figure was 38 percent less. Among women, a much different situation exists. Non-white women who were high school graduates earned, on the average, some 24 percent less than whites. Non-white female college graduates, however, earned but slightly over one percent less average annual salaries than white women college graduates. Significantly, the median annual income of non-white female college graduates was more than double that of non-white women with only (a) high school education.

Is it any wonder that among non-whites, as contrasted to whites, a larger proportion of women than of men attend and finish college? The lack of economic rewards for higher education goes far in accounting for the paucity of college graduates and the high rate of dropout among non-white males. It also accounts for the fact that in the North, where there are greater opportunities for white-collar negro males, more negro men than women are finishing college; whereas in the South, where teaching is the greatest employment outlet for negro college graduates, negro women college graduates outnumber men.

There is much in these situations that reflects the continuing matriarchal character of negro society – in a situation which had its roots in the family composition under slavery where the father, if identified, had no established role. Subsequent and continuing economic advantages of negro women who found steady employment as domestics during the post-Civil War era and thereafter perpetuated the pattern. This, in conjunction with easy access of white males to negro females, served to emasculate many negro men economically and psychologically. It also explains, in part, the high prevalence of broken homes, illegitimacy, and lack of motivation in the negro community.

The negro middle-class seems destined to grow and prosper. At the same time, the economic position of the untrained and poorly trained negro – as of all untrained and poorly trained in our society – will continue to decline. Non-whites are doubly affected. First, they are disproportionately concentrated in occupations particularly susceptible to unemployment at a time when our technology eats up unskilled and semi-skilled jobs at a frightening rate. Secondly, they are conditioned to racial job discrimination. The latter circumstance becomes a justification for not trying, occasioning a lack of incentive for self-betterment.

The tragedy of discrimination is that it provides an excuse for failure while erecting barriers to success.

Most colored Americans still are not only outside the mainstream of our society but see no hope of entering it. The champions of the status quo capitalize upon the lack of motivation and anti-social behavior, which result. They say that the average negro must demonstrate to the average white that the latter's fears are groundless. One proponent of this point of view has stated that negro crime and illegitimacy must decline and negro neighborhoods must stop deteriorating.

In these observations lie a volume on race relations. In the first place, those who articulate this point of view fail to differentiate between acceptance as earned by individual merit and enjoyment of rights guaranteed to everyone. Implicit, also, is the assumption that negroes can lift themselves by their bootstraps, and that once they become brown counterparts of white middle-class Americans, they will be accepted on the basis of individual merit. Were this true, our race problem would be no more than a most recent phase in the melting pot tradition of the nation.

As compared to the earlier newcomers to our cities from Europe, the later ones who are colored face much greater impediments in moving from the slums or from the bottom of the economic ladder. At the same time, they have less resources to meet the more difficult problems that confront them.

Exhibit E

One of the most obvious manifestations of the negro's paucity of internal resources is the absence of widespread integrated patterns of voluntary organizations. The latter, as we know, contributed greatly to the adjustment and assimilation of European immigrants. Both the negro's heritage and the nature of his migration in the United States mitigated against the development of similar institutions.

Slavery and resulting post-civil war dependence upon whites stifled self-reliance. Movement from the rural south to northern cities was a far cry from immigration from Europe to the new world. This internal migration was not an almost complete break with the past, nor were those who participated in it subjected to feelings of complete foreignness. Thus the negro tended to preserve his old institutions when he moved from one part of the nation to another; the immigrant created new ones. And most important, the current adjustment of non-whites to an urban environment is occurring at a time when public agencies are rapidly supplanting voluntary organizations.

Although much is written about crime and family disorganization among negroes, most literate Americans are poorly informed on such maters. The first fallacy that arises is a confusion of what racial crime figures reflect. When people read that negroes commit more than half the crime in a given community, they unconsciously translate this into an equally high proportion of negroes who are criminals. In fact, the latter proportion is extremely small.

In a similar vein, family stability, as indicated by the presence of both husband and wife, which is very low among the poorest non-whites, rises sharply as income increases. Equally revealing is the fact that, in all parts of the country, the proportion of non-white families with female heads falls as incomes rise. A good, steady paycheck appears to be an important element in family stability. Those negroes who have been able to improve their economic position have generally taken on many of the attributes of white middle-class Americans. But poverty still haunts half of the negroes in the United States, and while higher levels of national productivity are a sine qua non for higher levels of employment in the nation, they alone will not wipe out unemployment, especially for minorities. The labor reserve of today must be trained if it is to find gainful employment. Among non-whites, this frequently involves more than exposure to vocational training. Many of them are functionally illiterate and require basic education prior to any specialized job preparation.

The very magnitude of these problems illustrates that society must take the leadership in solving them. But society can only provide greater opportunities. The individual must respond to new opportunities. And he does so, primarily, in terms of visible evidence that hard work and sacrifice bring real rewards.

Many white Americans are perplexed, confused, and antagonized by negroes' persistent pressure to break down racial segregation. Few pause to consider what involuntary segregation means to its victims.

To the negro, as an American, involuntary segregation is degrading, inconvenient and costly. It is degrading because it is a tangible and constant reminder of the theory upon which it is based – biological and racial inferiority. It is inconvenient because it means long trips to work, exclusion from certain cultural and recreational facilities, lack of access to restaurants and hotels conveniently located, and frequently, relegation to grossly inferior accommodations. Sometimes it spells denial of a job and often it prevents upgrading based on ability.

But the principal disadvantage of involuntary segregation is its costliness. Nowhere is this better illustrated than in education and housing. By any and all criteria, separate schools are generally inferior schools in which the cultural deprivations of the descendants of slaves are perpetuated.

Enforced residential segregation, the most stubborn and universal of the negro's disadvantages, often leads to exploitation and effects a spatial pattern which facilitates neglect of public services in the well-defined areas where negroes live. It restricts the opportunities of the more successful as well as the least successful in the group, augmenting artificially the number of non-whites who live in areas of blight and neglect and face impediments to the attainment of values and behavior for upward social and economic mobility.

The most obvious consequence of involuntary residential segregation is that the housing dollar in a dark hand usually commands less purchasing power than one in a white hand. Clearly, this is a denial of a basic promise of a free economy.

For immigrant groups in the nation, the trend toward improved socioeconomic status has gone hand-in-hand with decreasing residential segregation. The reverse has been true of the negro. Eli Ginzberg, in his book, The Negro Potential, has delineated the consequences.

It must be recognized that the negro cannot suddenly take his proper place among whites in the adult world if he has never lived, played, and studied with them in childhood and young adulthood. Any type of segregation handicaps a person's preparation for work and life. . . Only when negro and white families can live together as neighbors. . . Will the negro grow up properly prepared for his place in the world of work.

Residential segregation based on color cannot be separated from residential segregation based upon income. Both have snob and class appeal in contemporary America. Concentration of higher income families in the suburbs means that many of those whose attitudes and values dominate our society do not see the poor or needy. But more important, cut off by political boundaries, it is to their interest not to see them.

Yet there are over 30,000,000 Americans who experience poverty today. For the most part, we resent them and the outlays required for welfare services. They are a group which is separate from the majority of Americans and for whom the latter accept only the minimum responsibility. Thus we have, for the first time, class unemployment in the United States.

I happen to have been born a negro and to have devoted a large part of my adult energies to the problem of the role of the negro in America. But I am also a government administrator, and have devoted just as much energy – if not more – to problems of government administration at the local, the state and the national level.

My responsibilities as a negro and an American are part of the heritage I received from my parents – a heritage that included a wealth of moral and social values that don't have anything to do with my race, either. My greatest difficulty in public life is combating the idea that somehow my responsibilities as a negro conflict with my responsibilities as a government administrator; and this is a problem which is represented by those negroes who feel that I represent them exclusively, as well as by those whites who doubt my capacity to represent all elements in the population. The fact is that my responsibilities as a negro and a government administrator do not conflict; they complement each other.

The challenge frequently thrown to me is why I don't go out into the negro community and exhort negro youths to prepare themselves for present and future opportunities. My answer is somewhat ambivalent. I know that emphasis upon values and behavior conducive to success in the dominant culture of America was an important part of my youthful training. But it came largely from my parents in the security and love of a middle-class family. (And believe me, nothing is more middle-class than a middle-class minority family!)

Many of the youth I am urged to exhort come from broken homes. They live in communities where the fellow who stays in school and follows the rules is a "square." They reside in a neighborhood where the most successful are often engaged in shady – if not illegal – activities. They know that the very policeman who may arrest them for violation of the law is sometimes the pay-off man for the racketeers. And they recognize that the majority society, which they frequently believe to be the "enemy", condones this situation. Their experience also leads some of them to believe that getting the kind of job the residents in the neighborhood hold is unrewarding – a commitment to hard work and poverty. For almost all of them, the precepts of Ben Franklin are lily-like in their applicability.

Included in the group is the third generation of welfare clients. It is in this area – where they learn all the jargon of the social workers and psychologists – that they demonstrate real creativity. It is in activities that "beat" the system that they are most adept – and where the most visible rewards are concentrated.

All youth is insecure today. Young people in our slums are not only insecure but also angry. Their horizons are limited, and, in withdrawing from competing in the larger society, they are creating a peculiar, but effective, feeling of something that approaches, of at least serves as a viable substitute for, security. In the process, new values and aspirations, a new vocabulary, a new standard of dress, and a new attitude toward authority evolve. Each of these serves to demonstrate a separateness from the dominant culture.

As a realist, I know that these youth relate with me primarily in a negative sense. They see me in terms of someone who has been able to penetrate, to a degree, the color line, and to them I have bettered the "enemy." If I should attempt to suggest their surmounting the restrictions of color, they cite instances of persons they know who were qualified – the relatively few boys or girls in their neighborhood who finished high school or even college – only to be ignored while white youths with much less training were selected for good jobs. And such occurrences are not unique or isolated in their experience.

The example which will be an inspiration to the negro boys and girls whose anti-social behavior distresses most whites and many negroes is someone they know who has experienced what they have experienced and has won acceptance in the mainstream of America. When the Ralph Bunches, William Hasties, and John Hope Franklins emerge from their environment, the achievements of these successful negroes will provide models that have meaning for them.

This is reflected in the occupations that provide the greatest incidence of mobility for slum youth. One thinks immediately of prize fighting and jazz music. In these fields there is a well-established tradition of negroes, reared in the ghetto areas of blight and poverty, who have gone to the top. For youth in a similar environment, these are heroes with whom they can and do identify and relate. And in these fields, a significant proportion of the successful are non-whites. For only in those pursuits in which native genius can surmount (if indeed it does not profit from) lack of high-level training does the dominant environment of the negro facilitate large-scale achievement.

For many successful older colored Americans, middle-class status has been difficult. Restricted, in large measure, to racial ghettos, they have expended great effort to protect their children from falling back into the dominant values of that environment. And these values are probably more repugnant to them than to most Americans. This is understandable in terms of their social origins. For the most part, they come from lower-middle class families where industry, good conduct, family ties, and a willingness to postpone immediate rewards for future successes are stressed. Their values and standards of conduct are those of success-oriented middle-class Americans.

It is not that responsible negroes fail to feel shame about muggings, illegitimacy, and boisterousness on the part of other negroes. Many – particularly the older ones – feel too much shame in this connection. Accordingly, some either repudiate the "culprits" in terms of scathing condemnation or try to escape from the problem lest it endanger their none too secure status.

These attitudes, too, are shifting. The younger middle-class negroes are more secure and consequently place less stress upon the quest for respectability. But few negroes are immune from the toll of upward mobility. Frequently, their struggle has been difficult, and the

Exhibit E

maintenance of their status demands a heavy input. As long as this is true, they will have less energy to devote to the problems of the negro subculture. It is significant, however, that the sit-ins and freedom marches in the south were planned and executed by negro college students, most of whom come from middle-class families. Middle-class negroes have long led the fight for civil rights; today its youthful members do not hesitate to resort to direct action, articulating the impatience that is rife throughout the negro community. In so doing, they are forging a new solidarity in the struggle for human dignity.

There are today, as there always have been, thousand of dedicated colored Americans who don't make the headlines but are successful in raising the horizons of negroes. These are the less well-known leaders who function at the local level. The teachers, social workers, local political leaders, ministers, doctors, and an assortment of indigenous leaders – many among the latter with little formal education – who are effective (and) have familiarized themselves with the environmental factors which dull and destroy motivation. They become involved with the total negro community. They demonstrate – rather than verbalize – a concern for negro youth's problems. They are trying to reach these young people, not by coddling and providing excuses for failure, but through identification of their potentialities and assistance in the development of these. Involved are both genuine affection and sufficient toughness to facilitate and encourage the development of self-reliance.

Those, white and black alike, who reach the newcomers in our urban areas avoid value judgments relative to cultural patterns. When they suggest thrift, good deportment, greater emphasis upon education and training, they do so as a pragmatic approach. For them, it is not a matter of proselytizing, but in a matter of delineating those values and patterns of behavior that accelerate upward mobility in American society. Such a sophisticated approach enables them to identify deviations from dominant values and conduct which are not inconsistent with a productive and healthy life in modern urban communities. The latter are left undisturbed, so that there will be a minimum adjustment of values and concepts and the maximum functional effectiveness on the part of individuals who will not soon become middle-class America.

What are the responsibilities of negro leadership?

Certainly, the first is to keep pressing for first-class citizenship status – an inevitable goal of those who accept the values of this nation.

Another responsibility of negro leadership is to encourage and assist negroes to prepare for the opportunities that are now and will be opened to them.

The ultimate responsibilities of negro leadership, however, are to show results and maintain a following. This means that it cannot be so "responsible" that it forgets the trials and tribulations of others who are less fortunate or less recognized than itself. It cannot stress progress – the emphasis that is so palatable to the majority group – without, at the same time, delineating the unsolved business of democracy. It cannot provide or identify meaningful models unless it effects social changes that facilitate the emergence of these models from the environment, which typifies so much of the negro community.

But negro leadership must also face up to the deficiencies which plague the negro community, and it must take effective action to deal with resulting problems. While, of course, crime, poverty, illegitimacy and hopelessness can all be explained, in large measure, in terms of the negro's history and current status in America, they do exist. We need no longer be self-conscious in admitting these unpleasant facts, for our knowledge of human behavior indicates clearly that anti-social activities are not inherent in any people. What is required is comprehension of these – a part of society's problems – and remedial and rehabilitation measures.

Emphasis upon self-betterment, if employed discriminately by negro leaders, is seized upon by white supremacists and their apologists to support the assertion that negroes – and they mean all negroes – are not ready for full citizenship. This, because of the nature of our society, negro leadership must continue to stress rights if it is to receive a hearing for programs of self-improvement.

Black Muslims, who identify the white man as the devil, can and do emphasize – with a remarkable degree of success – morality, industry, and good conduct. But, the negro leader who does not repudiate his or his followers' Americanism can do so effectively only as he, too, clearly repudiates identification with white supremacists. This he does, of course, when he champions equal rights, just as the black Muslims accomplish it by directing hate toward all white people.

Most negroes in leadership capacities have articulated the fact that they and those who follow them are a part of America. They have striven for realization of the American dream. Most recognize their responsibilities as citizens and urge others to follow their example. Sophisticated whites realize that the status of negroes in our society depends not only upon what the negro does to achieve his goals and prepare himself for opportunities but, even more, upon what all America does to expand these opportunities. And the quality and nature of future negro leadership depends upon how effective those leaders who relate to the total society can be in satisfying the yearnings for human dignity that reside in the hearts of all Americans.

The Essential Documents of American History was compiled by Norman P. Desmarais and James H. McGovern of Providence College.

REFERENCES

PREFACE

The Olathe Daily News, Olathe, KS, 2005

CHAPTER 2

Essential Documents in American History 1492–Present, Great Neck Publishing, accessed through EBSCO Publishing 2005.

Ogletree, Charles J., <u>All Deliberate Speed: Reflections on the First Half-Century of Brown v. Board of Education</u> (W.W. Norton & Co., 2004)

The Columbia Electronic Encyclopedia, 2005.

Letson, John W., *In Atlanta Schools (NEA Journal, 1963)*

Congressional Record 84th Congress, 1956

Our Georgia History (http://ourgeorgiahistory.com) c 2001–2005 by Golden Ink

Chalmers, David, <u>Hooded Americanism: The History of the Ku Klux Klan,</u> Third Edition,1981, Duke University Press, Durham, NC, 1987.

Quarles, Chester L., <u>The Ku Klux Klan and Related American Racialist and Antisemitic Organizations: A History and Analysis</u>, McFarland & Company, Inc., Publishers, Jefferson, NC and London, 1999

Ingalls, Robert P., <u>Hoods: The Story of the Ku Klux Klan</u>, G.P. Putnam's Sons, New York, 1979) as cited by Chester L. Quarles

Pitts, Leonard, copyright 2005, *Miami Herald*

References

Kennedy, Stetson, The Klan Unmasked, Florida Atlantic University Press, Boca Raton, FL, 1990

1996–2004 City Directory, (http://www.city-directory.com/Overview/history/history6.htm) accessed 2005

Rice, Arnold S. The Ku Klux Klan in American Politics, Public Affairs Press, Washington, D.C., 1962 as cited by Quarles

Intimidation, Reprisal and Violence in the South's Racial Crisis, 1959.

Retrenchment and Redirection (1950–1959), Atlanta Regional Consortium for Higher Education, 2004, (http://www.atlantahighered.org/civilrights/essay) Accessed 2005.

CHAPTER 3

Johnson, Charles and Adelman, Bob, KING: The photobiography of Martin Luther King, Jr., Viking Studio, New York, NY, 2000

CHAPTER 4

Historic West End: The Story of West End and a Walking Tour Guide, West End Neighborhood Development, c Wend, Atlanta, GA, 1981

CHAPTER 5

McClain, Roy, This Way Please: Facing Life's Crossroads, Fleming H. Revell Company, Wetwood, NJ, 1957

Chalmers, <u>Hooded Americanism: The History of the Ku Klux Klan</u>, Third Edition, 1981, Duke University Press, Durham, NC, 1987

Quarles, Chester L., <u>The Ku Klux Klan and Related American Racialist and Antisemitic Organizations: A History and Analysis</u>, McFarland & Company, Inc., Publishers, Jefferson, NC and London, 1999

Jones, III, Bishop Bevel L, <u>One Step Beyond Caution: Reflections on Life and Faith</u>, Looking Glass Books, Decatur GA, 2001

Personal files of Dr. Dow Kirkpatrick as provided by Rev. Jimmy Moor, Senior Pastor, St. Mark United Methodist Church, Atlanta, GA

King, Martin Luther, Sr. with Clayton Riley, William Morrow and Company, Inc. New York, 1980

Harwell, Jack U., <u>Louie D.: A Photographic Essay of "Mr. Baptist," Louie DeVotie Newton,</u> The Christian Index, Atlanta, GA, 1979

CHAPTER 6

<u>Background Atlanta: A Handbook for Reporters covering the desegregation of Atlanta Public Schools,</u> OASIS Organizations Assisting Schools in September, Atlanta, GA, 1961

Larrabee, Brandon, <u>In Georgia, gains – and some retreats since landmark integration ruling</u>, Morris News Service, Athens Banner-Herald and Morris Digital Works, 2004

Phase Three – Direct Action & Desegregation (1960–1965), Atlanta Regional Consortium for Higher Education, 2004, (http://www.atlantahighered.org/civilrights/essay) Accessed 2005.

Hein, Virginia H., The Image of "A City Too Busy to Hate": Atlanta in the 1960's, *Phylon: The Atlanta University Review of Race and Culture*, Third Quarter 1972

Public Papers of John F. Kennedy, American Reference Library.

Sarratt, Reed, The Ordeal of Desegregation: The first decade, Harper & Row, 1966

CHAPTER 7

Koinonia Partners, (http://www.koinoniapartners.org) Accessed 2005

King, Martin Luther, Sr. with Clayton Riley, Daddy King: An Autobiography, William Morrow and Company, Inc. New York, 1980

David Van Biema, Alice Jackson Baughn, David Thigpen, Deirdre van Dyk, *Time*, 5/24/2004

Kennedy, Stetson, The Klan Unmasked, Florida Atlantic University Press, Boca Raton, FL, 1990

CHAPTER 9

Short, Bob, Everything is Pickrick: The Life of Lester Maddox, Mercer University Press, Macon, GA 1999

Maddox, Lester Garfield, Speaking Out: the Autobiography of Lester Garfield Maddox, Doubleday & Company, Inc., Garden City, NY 1975

Jacobs, Hal, Lester, *Creative Loafing*, 1999, citation obtained at (http://www.artery.org/Maddox-CL.htm) Accessed 2006.

CHAPTER 10

Ngeorgia.com
(http://ngeorgia.com/attractions/stonemountaincarving.com)
Accessed 2006

Chalmers, <u>Hooded Americanism: The History of the Ku Klux Klan</u>, Third Edition, 1981, Duke University Press, Durham, NC, 1987

Southern Poverty Law Center, *Pontifex, Esq.?* Intelligence Report, Spring 1999,
(http://www.splcenter.org/intel/intelreport/article.jsp?aid=35
4) c 2005, Accessed 2006

CHAPTER 11

Essential Documents in American History 1492–Present, Great Neck Publishing, accessed through EBSCO Publishing 2005.

Diuguid, Lewis W., <u>A Teacher's Cry</u>, Universal Publishers, Boca Raton, FL 2004

CHAPTER 12

Starling, Kelly, *Ebony,* October 1998, c 1998 Johnson Publishing Co.